Cambridge Elements ≡

Elements in the Philosophy of Law
edited by
George Pavlakos
University of Glasgow
Gerald J. Postema
University of North Carolina at Chapel Hill
Kenneth M. Ehrenberg ·
University of Surrey

THE MATERIALITY OF THE LEGAL ORDER

Marco Goldoni
University of Glasgow

CAMBRIDGE
UNIVERSITY PRESS

CAMBRIDGE
UNIVERSITY PRESS

University Printing House, Cambridge CB2 8BS, United Kingdom

One Liberty Plaza, 20th Floor, New York, NY 10006, USA

477 Williamstown Road, Port Melbourne, VIC 3207, Australia

314–321, 3rd Floor, Plot 3, Splendor Forum, Jasola District Centre,
New Delhi – 110025, India

103 Penang Road, #05–06/07, Visioncrest Commercial, Singapore 238467

Cambridge University Press is part of the University of Cambridge.

It furthers the University's mission by disseminating knowledge in the pursuit of
education, learning, and research at the highest international levels of excellence.

www.cambridge.org
Information on this title: www.cambridge.org/9781009009669
DOI: 10.1017/9781009000499

First published 2022

A catalogue record for this publication is available from the British Library.

ISBN 978-1-009-00966-9 Paperback
ISSN 2631-5815 (online)
ISSN 2631-5807 (print)

The Materiality of the Legal Order

Elements in the Philosophy of Law

DOI: 10.1017/9781009000499
First published online: April 2022

Marco Goldoni
University of Glasgow

Author for correspondence: Marco Goldoni, Marco.Goldoni@glasgow.ac.uk

Abstract: This Element aims to explore how the relation between societal organisation and legal order – the question of materiality – has been investigated in philosophy of law. The starting point of the Element is that such relation has often been left invisible or thematised in poor and reductive terms. After explaining the main reasons behind this neglect, the Element provides an overview of the three main approaches to legal philosophy whose contributions, though not always effective, can still provide some insights for a contemporary analysis of legal order's materiality: materialism, legal institutionalism, and the new materialism. The last section of the Element suggests looking for a footing for the study of materiality in two fields: the metaphysics of relations and the political economy of legal orders.

Keywords: legal institutionalism, law of political economy, Marxism, new materialism, materiality relation

ISBNs: 9781009009669 (PB), 9781009000499 (OC)
ISSNs: 2631-5815 (online), 2631-5807 (print)

Contents

1 The Materiality Question

The title of this Element indicates the object of its study. The drive to focus on the material dimension of the legal order is dictated by a timely concern, that is, the impulse to understand the legal relations that pertain to the contemporary political economy. This angle has taken up a new and urgent configuration with three of the most dangerous crises of this century's first two decades: the financial and economic crisis of 2008, the Covid-19 pandemic, and the incipient environmental catastrophe. These issues have made the question of the materiality of law more pressing than ever. Yet, articulating the legal order within the perimeter of a concrete social and economic organisation is part and parcel of a more general enquiry into the connection between fundamental social relations and the activity of legal ordering through institutions and other non-institutional factors. That connection instantiates what could be defined as the 'materiality relation', the invariable aspect in it being that it concerns (fundamental) aspects of the social order and its reproduction. What the nature of that relation is and what its relata are remain controversial issues. One of the main problems is that the question has only intermittently been addressed in legal philosophy. For a proper reappraisal, it is necessary to analyse the nature and the features of the materiality relation. In other words, how does the legal order relate to its constituents? This Element won't provide a definitive answer to this question, but it will articulate the range of relata that have been employed in the explanation of legal order's formation and then propose a research agenda. Hence, it seems appropriate to start by reconstructing how the idea of materiality has been either excised from legal reasoning or conceived often in non-material terms (because the constituent social facts have been described in non-material terms), and not only in domestic legal theory but also within transnational legal theory.

The starting point of the enquiry is to explain how the dominant ways of conceiving of the emergence of the legal order within society have often excluded the question of its material organisation, that is, its constituent materials. This section will broach three of the main devices for explaining the relation between societal formation and legal ordering (via the constitution of legal authority). These are political theories whose explanatory power has exercised an enormous grip on the imagination of legal theorists. They are mostly responsible for establishing the frame for thinking about the rise of the legal order and its unfolding. In this way, they have set the scene for mainstream legal theories and how they conceive of their content while underplaying their societal dimension. Such obfuscation has been realised in two ways: either through the assumption that the processes of social organisation involved in shaping the legal order would remain external to that order or through the idea that law would establish its authority on a basis that has nothing to do with its social underpinnings, only with constitutive principles. In the first case, an abstraction – usually, assuming the existence of officials (Roughan, 2019) – allows the theorist to ignore the material dimension of the legal order. In the second case, the legal order is supposed to bootstrap the material dimension into existence. In either way, the question of what we will call the materiality relation is marginalised when not left completely invisible.

In order to grasp the theoretical origins of this exclusion from legal thinking, it is important to recap how political philosophies have allowed or even realised the displacement of materiality with some of their most influential notions. As we shall see, part of the problem that concerns both political and legal philosophy is a certain obsession with the order's origin. In particular, the removal of materiality is often dictated by the first move of the theory: locating the origin outside of the social and legal orders is a way of obscuring how the material organisation of society has been productive of order or is, at least, imbricated within the order in a way that cannot be easily ignored.

The first of these theories is possibly the most important modern political conception of the genesis of the social and legal order: the social contract. According to this theoretical device, the social and then the legal order are brought about through a hypothetical or real agreement by all the subjects of the social order itself. As is known, in the most common versions of the social contract the legal order emerges against the background of the state of nature, which is portrayed as a pre-socialised state where it is rational for agents to intend to escape it. Whether it is a dangerous place as in Hobbes' conception or a milder but uncertain state as in Locke's, it does not matter for the determination of the social contract's function. In this fictional state of nature, co-operation is either unnatural or extremely fragile, and certainly insufficient. Accordingly, the question that drives the formation of the social contract is deeply shaped by this precarious condition. In other and more mature versions, when the state of nature is openly formalised as an epistemic device (for example, the original position as it is in Rawls' first phase), it is presented as a way to assess our ethical theories and their underlying assumptions (Rawls, 1971, s. 3). In both cases, interests are rightly put at the centre of social formation, but the whole point (and leverage) of the social contract is that it provides a solution for the protection of certain interests that are deemed to be formed already in the pre-social phase. In this way, the relational formation of interests is obliterated and the main aspects of the organisation of the social order are defined on the basis of an abstraction that does not know of any process of socialisation. The legal order and its objectives are also conceived as being external to the process of socialisation.

The problem for legal theory is that this fiction is fabricated in a way that displaces the role of constitutive social relations. In fact, the social relations that pertain at the time of the so-called origin (whether the state of nature or the original position) are then concealed, nullified by virtue of a thought experiment, but one that acts as a distorting lens because it de-politicises existing material conditions and social relations. Once translated into legal theory, the social contract also provides the frame for taking matters out of the ordinary political and social processes of contestation. In other words, the material aspect of the legal order is entirely (and deliberately) concealed from view at the very important point of societal formation and organisation. The political theory of the social contract is then one that rationalises the relation between the rise of the social order and the formation of the legal order as a relation of separation. Accordingly, the reasons for having a political association – more concretely, for having *that specific* political association – can be left outside of the development of the legal order because they do not form part of the legal fabric. The social contract is a device for theorising the irrelevance of co-operation and interaction (i.e., social organisation) for the formation of the legal order. Strangely enough, this is a device that, at least in certain versions, is supposed to give moral reasons for entering into society (cf. Rousseau, 1994). But the logic of contract – if truly contractarian – is usually one of predetermined self-interest. As noted by a prominent critic: 'Those who enter contracts typically are concerned with their own benefits and need not care about the benefits to their partners in trade' (Hardin, 2013, p. 23). It is not relevant for the topic of this section whether social contract thinking is the most effective way of dealing with issues of collective co-ordination and the composition of different interests. In its own terms, it might be. But it is essential to note that placing the origin of the social order outside of the legal order leaves its materiality outside of legal knowledge.

From the perspective of the social contract, constitutionalising certain principles and rights is admitted as a device to keep the order together (say, for example, with the constitutionalisation of the maximin principle), by protecting some of the interests that allegedly existed already before their entry into society. But the point of observation provided by the social contract does not allow us to question the modality of formation of the order and does not provide an understanding of how it was formed or what was, in that process, the role of the legal order. The legal order is basically introduced by the social contract, but it remains external to social relations. Rather, it is applied to social relations as law comes to be seen as an instrument of protection of already established social roles and functions.

The most important alternative to the social contract tradition is represented by the conventionalist approach. This is one of the most developed and sophisticated explanations and justifications of legal orders and particularly of liberal-democratic orders (for a classic defence, see Hardin, 1999). Since at least the publication of David Hume's work, the idea that the organisation of society and the creation of a government are the products of a social convention has been acquiring a lot of traction. In recent times, the study of conventionalism has been revived by David Lewis (1969), who has provided an extensive analysis of what a convention is. In legal and political theory, the idea has become prominent after having been taken up first by H. L. A. Hart (1994) and then by Gerald Postema (1982) and by Andrei Marmor (2008). Furthermore, the idea has gained enormous influence for two reasons. First, conventions are an apt device for explaining the co-ordination necessary to achieve the complex organisation of pluralist societies. As they do not exercise a mandatory force on the basis of substantial reasons, conventions provide a useful point of convergence for different perspectives and values without frustrating the expectations of each agent in an unreasonable way. In fact, according to the classic understanding, a convention is followed mainly because other people follow it (Postema, 1982, p. 167). To follow a convention is to engage in a common form of behaviour and to meet the expectations of others, while having expectations oneself regarding the behaviour of others (Spaak, 2018, p. 334). In other words, a convention can solve problems of co-ordination,[1] deep disagreement, and game-theory challenges in a more effective way than the social contract device. It does not entail the demanding expectation of a general and explicit agreement on all the essentials of the legal order.

The biggest influence of conventionalism can be seen in the impact made by a conventionalist reading of the rule of recognition in contemporary legal theory. As is known, Hart himself (1994, p. 255) came to endorse that interpretation of the rule of recognition in his postscript. The relevance of this approach to legal theory for the current section is evident. One could study the connections among politics, law, and the economy as existing in an equilibrium set by certain conventions among legal officials. This is not a taxing conception as it does not mobilise the substantial norms of a constitutional order (or, at least, not directly). But, precisely for these reasons, it does not capture the ground of the legal order, either.[2] This is not surprising because the deeper the agreement on the point of a common behaviour, the higher the probability that there will be conflict or

---

[1] Postema (1982, p. 197) is the most explicit in stating that there are at least three levels of co-ordination: between citizens; between citizens and officials; and between officials.

[2] For a different reading that tries to adapt the rule of recognition to the metaphysics of grounding and anchoring, see Epstein (2015, ch. 7).

disagreement. However, it is possible to imagine that the conventionalist explanation of the legal order might come across as compatible with the material study of it, suggesting an understanding of the rule of recognition as the articulation of the materiality relation. The possibility of reading the rule of recognition as the coupling between the positive and the social normativity of law confirms that this would not be an eccentric move. For this reason, it is worth unpacking further the notion of a conventional rule of recognition. According to one of the most prominent theorists of the conventional rule of recognition, Andrei Marmor (2008, pp. 14–15), all conventional rules respect two conditions: a condition of *dependency* and a condition of *arbitrariness*. The former postulates that one of the reasons for following a convention is that others do the same. A group of people follow a rule R if they have certain reasons to follow it. But the members of the group do not have to follow the rule because of those reasons. As Joseph Raz (1990, p. 178) puts it, 'they must conform to the rule but they do not need to comply with it'. Marmor implies that members of the group do not even need to be aware of the reasons so that their obligation *depends* on the compliance of the others. The rule of recognition instantiates these features in its most visible form because it links political and social morality with authoritative normativity. As Marmor reminds us, the reasons to obey the law belong to moral considerations, but these considerations cannot be inferred or derived 'from the norms that determine what the law is' (Marmor, 2011, p. 152).

The second condition assumes that there is an element of arbitrariness in the choice of convention. The conventional rule can be arbitrary (i.e., it could have been otherwise) even if it reflects moral or political convictions (Marmor, 2001, p. 21). Ultimately, it is the rule-following behaviour that makes it a conventional rule more than its substantial content. The reason for following conventional rules is adhesion to the convention of the relevant agents. In other words, the key organising factor of the legal order is conventional, while other substantial principles and aims enter the picture only if allowed and introjected via the fundamental social convention. The social convention on which the order is based, while different in its driving logic from the social contract because it assumes that the convergence operates through adjustment of expectations, shares with the social contract the fact that the constitutive rules of the legal order do not make reference to the organisation of social relations. In brief, although not indifferent to co-operation and the function of socialisation of interests and expectations, the conventionalist view does not thematise these as the main reasons behind the formation of the convention. The social convention is a way to solve the problems generated by issues of co-ordination, co-operation, and conflict of interests, but always from a position external to the content of social relations.

A common alternative to the previous two approaches is represented by the social and political theories that focus on the symbolic origins of the legal and social order. The gist of these political theories as currently used in legal and sociological studies is typically modern and advances the idea that social orders in the age of the state are formed around an ordering principle like that of sovereignty (see Loughlin, 2003, ch. 5). Unlike contract or convention, sovereignty mobilises a different type of motivation and cannot be explained simply in terms of game theory or co-ordination issues. Its political psychology makes the principle of sovereignty rather different from these other alternative explanatory devices. Individual interest is not the main motive behind the principle of sovereignty. In fact, the dimension addressed by sovereignty is not primarily the negotiation or bargaining between interests or the rational deliberation about the best design for a community's legal order. Rather, it is a particular achievement, the general will, that puts into motion collective political action. This achievement is not parasitical on a previous pre-political arrangement because it makes the rise of the political sphere the key moment of community formation and provides symbolic access to a dimension of political meaning. This is already evident in Rousseau's conception of sovereignty and his emphasis on the discontinuity between the principle of sovereignty and government. According to Rousseau (1994), forming a sovereign political community entails giving up one's natural rights in order to receive back the goods of the civil condition. This is a process that radically changes the participants. Unlike the previous strategies of explanation about the formation of the social and legal order, contract and convention, the emergence of sovereignty in Rousseau requires indeed a transformation of the individual from private person to citizen. In the end, the logic at play in the institution of a sovereign association is everything but contractual: '[N]othing is truly renounced by private individuals under the social contract ... [I]nstead of abandoning anything[,] they have simply made a beneficial transfer, exchanging an uncertain and precarious mode of existence for a better and more secure one, natural independence for liberty, the power of hurting others for their own safety' (Rousseau, 1994, p. 70).

Contrary to how it might appear prima facie, this is not contractualist thinking. In Rousseau's social contract there is much more than the deployment of strategic rationality. The exit from the state of nature is led by recognition of the common interest. The complete alienation of one's rights brings about nothing less than a profound change in the subject. The logic of association entails the acquisition of moral status via the concept of the general will. Sovereignty is then manifested through the exercise of the general will and for this reason cannot be represented or transferred. The distinction between sovereignty and government derives from this notion of the general will. Rousseau is worried about the extension of government's powers not because he wants to protect individual autonomy but because the expansion of governmental reach might encroach upon the sovereign and limit its powers. Government can only apply and implement the law through decrees and decisions, but the set-up of the political community is a competence of the sovereign and its general will.

What is of interest here is the different logic undergirding this important tradition of sovereignty, one that identifies its order-generative capacity in a dynamic that is not of strict reciprocity but is still normatively oriented towards equality. The association generates more power than is given up by subjects; it also socialises interests, making possible the emergence of the general will over the will of all. In this way, sovereignty is productive of social co-operation and order. Another non-contractual mode of conceiving of the emergence of the social order as a sovereign device begins not with interest but with desire, and it operates according to the logic of political sacrifice. It is possible to identify a powerful exemplification of such a sacrificial logic in the work of René Girard (1972). His starting point is neither the pre-political interest of social contract thinking nor the indifference to reasons typical of the conventionalist approach, but desire and its mimetic nature, by which Girard means the logic of reproduction of desire, a logic based on the tendency to imitate someone else's desire. In brief, human beings are desiring animals, but they do not know what they want to desire. Hence, desire is generated by imitation, that is, through the mediation of a model. By definition, multiple desires over the same object cannot all be satisfied and this fact might generate rivalry. Manufacturing the social order out of this condition is demanding because rivalry can quickly escalate into violence and open up a cycle of revenge. Only a sacrificial action, according to Girard, can interrupt the cycle of violence engendered by mimetic desire and potential revenge. This is made possible by the individuation of the scapegoat, which is produced by 'a deliberate act of collective substitution performed at the expense of the victim and absorbing all the internal tensions, feuds, and rivalries pent up within the community' (Girard, 1972, p. 31).[3] At its core, this is a non-reciprocal logic the aim of which is to contain and channel the latent unleashing of social violence intrinsic to mimetic desire. The aim is obtained by choosing a victim

---

[3] Sacrifice becomes the political device for protecting the legal order from its own violence: 'The sacrifice serves to protect the entire community from its own violence; it prompts the entire community to choose victims outside itself' (Girard, 1972, p. 32). One of the problems of Girard's account is that it implies that sacrifice is an anthropological feature of all social orders, as it is the origin of the social bond. But this is an overly inclusive claim.

(or, in another version, an enemy) that is within the community, but at a just distance from the rest of it.[4] The outcome of this process of victimisation produces a sacred and symbolic dimension with ordering capacity (Wydra, 2015, pp. 1–18). But this is far from being only a limitation of violence within the community (although it is an important containment); it also participates in the constitution of the social order by instituting a symbolic sphere. Girard's intuition, however, has been given a twist by modern legal theorists. Instead of looking into the rational choice and preference-based types of explanation or justification of the political community, this type of political anthropology puts exposure to sacrifice as a constitutive aspect of ancient and modern associations. But, unlike Girard's version, the possibility of sacrificing is not part of a process of victimisation. Rather, it is an act with which a subject *sacrifices something for* the existence or preservation of the legal order. As brilliantly described by Moshe Halbertal (2011, p. 55), this means that in modern legal orders the sacrificial logic takes the form of 'sacrificing for' rather than the ancient practice of 'sacrificing to'.

The potential unevenness that lies at the core of the social order is owing to the exposure of people (willingly or unwillingly) to sacrifice for the sake of the creation or maintenance of the legal order (Kahn, 2004, ch. 5). The legal order is portrayed as the formalisation of a certain political dynamic, but, even more importantly, its existence remains dependent not only on the political willingness to invest at least potentially the body politic with a sacrificial economy, often in the form of conscription, but also on exposure to potential mass destruction as is the case with terrorism and nuclear weapons (for an influential take, see Agamben, 1998).

This position offers a powerful critique of the idea that a political association is a contractual mechanism or a conventionalist procedure. But the *pars construens* is less convincing and leaves the function of holding a political community together to an impalpable and flimsy concept like political will. At best, this approach approximates a version of political theology that is helpful in providing a critique of the formalism affecting the social contract tradition and conventionalism by emphasising the necessary symbolic dimension of the social order. But it severs the connection between the symbolic and how society is organised while making access to the symbolic dimension transcendental. Perhaps it is also true that the sacrificial logic behind it can trigger a form of legal imagination in virtue of its capacity to reach the

---

[4] For this reason, sacrifice can be ritualised and obtaining the right distance from the community becomes one of the objectives of the ritual. If the distance were not enough, the sacrifice would just trigger another cycle of violent revenges and if it were too much, the sacrifice would fail to register as such and would qualify as a crime.

symbolic level, but it is not clear why this would be the only available associative logic or why it would shape a legal order into a concrete form (Girard, 1986). Anthropologically, it is questionable to state that political sacrifice is the necessary and unavoidable feature that generates authentic and stable social ordering. The sacrificial argument, usually employed against market fundamentalists and instrumentalists of almost any sort, does not enjoy anthropological universal validity.

Nor it is clear why it is always the case that sacrifice represents the cornerstone of political commitment. As noted by Wendy Brown (2015, pp. 213–14), 'sacrificing for' can also become a device for hampering imagination when it is associated with economics-driven rationality. As Brown remarks, the sacrificial device can be turned on its head and become a shared sacrifice for the sake of only some parts of the community or, in the case of the rhetoric about austerity, for economic growth. For example, this is the logic undergirding the recent constitutionalisation of austerity (cf. Christodoulidis 2021, ss. 3.2 and 3.3). But this last instantiation cannot be fully grasped if sacrifice is understood as generative first of all of a symbolic dimension. As it is for social contract thinking, in this version sovereignty belongs to an extraordinary moment that remains external to the ordinary organisation of social relations. It sets them into motion by remaining external to them, hence the possibility of imagining that the principle of sovereignty can transcend civil society. The material aspect works rather as a bearer of the extraordinary function of sovereignty, but, although it invests citizens' bodies, it does so as a marker and not as a principle of social organisation. Rather than remaining anchored to untenably vague notions of life and body, charisma and sovereignty, the rationality of the principle of sovereignty is better grasped when attached to processes of social differentiation and organisation. In the end, the coupling between sovereignty and sacrifice clearly invests a material dimension, but political theology reduces sacrifice to a mark on the body of the citizen. This view fails to capture the ordering properties of sovereignty. There is no visible and clear relation between exposing the body to political sacrifice and a specific organisation of the legal order, unless the theory contents itself with a reconstruction of the mystical foundation of authority. This approach might be able to explain the symbolic dimension of the legal order, but certainly not its materiality, and one is left wondering whether it would be enough to understand the identity of the order.

The uneven and non-reciprocal aspects of the conception of sovereignty illustrated so far nonetheless contain some precious insights, in particular the idea that the formation of the legal order does not need to postulate any fictitious equal exchange. The process of social organisation tends to be based (though not exclusively) on a distribution of roles and functions, which can be driven by patterns of reciprocity or of other nature (see Polanyi, 2001, ch. 3). The materiality of the legal order is given shape around these focal points of social organisation. Specifically, in modern times, the process of societal formation has been driven by differentiation and specialisation (Thornhill, 2011; Christodoulidis, 2022; and, for a different and 'hybrid' view, Latour, 2006). Because of these traits, it is necessary to limit certain claims concerning the materiality of the legal order only to modern legal experiences, that is, orders that have reached a certain level of complexity and functional specialisation. Accordingly, it is also better to avoid over-generalising claims about universal and exclusive ordering factors for each and every society. In a context of growing complexity and interdependence, the organisation of fundamental aspects of societal formation is a condition of existence and development that cannot easily go unnoticed. Unlike other political theories concerning the origins of order, a material perspective entails an *immanent* view. In other words, an analysis of the materiality relation should begin with the assumption that seeds of the legal order are already contained in patterns of social organisation: not as an effect of it, neither as a condition of possibility of that same social organisation. Rather, the legal order is immanent to social organisation.[5] *Organisation* and *relations* emerge as the twin objects of analysis for understanding the processes of how materiality migrates into the legal order. The moulding of social and legal orders is thus understood as a process of (according to the different perspectives) production, integration, assemblage, and composition (this is not intended to be an exhaustive list).

The second key move for approaching the materiality of the legal order without resorting to unique ordering methods is to focus the attention primarily on the *ordinary* processes of societal formation. Once the emphasis moves from the exception to normality, the possibility of accessing the materiality of the legal order becomes more concrete. The relation of materiality takes up its form not during exceptional moments but on an ordinary basis and with a view to finding a relatively stable and, indeed, *normal* order. The centre of this conception is the organisation of social relations that allows society to produce and reproduce itself. With a different terminology, it is legitimate to state that the organisation of society is the moulding of a set of social relations of which law is certainly an important subsystem, but not the only one. As already noted, the key starting point is that certain social relations are fundamental for the formation of a society, but they do not remain outside of it once society is formed. This means that the unfolding of certain modern phenomena (e.g., a society's

---

[5] The modern classic position in political philosophy is put forward in Spinoza (2000).

political economy, its modern science, its technology, its relationship with religion) is fundamental for the production and reproduction of the social order itself. Some of these relations also contain principles or rules of legal ordering. It is one of the most important tasks of legal philosophy to understand the nature of those relations, and other disciplines might also be extremely helpful (e.g., the contemporary debate on the metaphysics of relations is certainly relevant for an accurate description of those relations: Marmodoro & Yates, 2016; see Section 5 of this Element). The two points made in this section (immanent organisation and the prominence of normality) can be declined in different ways, but they function as crucial vectors of legal knowledge. In other words, broaching the question of organising the production and reproduction of a social order and placing the level of analysis on the stabilisation of normality are necessary operations for addressing the materiality relation from the juridical point of view.

In the rest of this Element, the objective is to focus selectively on some of the most important streams of thought that have given pride of place to the material dimension of law with a view to showing their insightful contributions and, at the same time, their weaknesses. These approaches have engaged extensively with the relation between the material and the form of law, or (on a different level) between social and legal organisation. But in the modern history of legal thought, the question of the material dimension of the legal order has not been thematised very frequently. The two classic approaches to legal theory, legal positivism and natural law theory, have almost always avoided confronting the material dimension of law *qua* question of legal analysis, and have been satisfied with a generic link to social facts (as in the conventionalist version, for example) or to the over-determining force of morality. For this reason, the focus will be on streams of legal thought more sensitive to the material organisation of society.

Unsurprisingly, the notion of materiality has been understood in different ways by non-materialist approaches as well. As already mentioned, by referring to materiality in this Element the intention is to capture the internal relation between societal formation and legal ordering. Under this aspect, the reconstruction provided in the following sections will not address those approaches that put emphasis on or give prominence to the autonomy of the form of the law. This is not because those are not useful for understanding the materiality of the legal order. To the contrary: some of these approaches have addressed the material dimension of the legal order (i.e., its legal identity) by beginning from the formal dimension and have put forward insightful perspectives on the concept of the legal system. Kelsen's idea of the constitution in the material sense represents a perfect example of that type of contribution (see Vinx, 2021).

In a legal system made up of a hierarchy of norms, those norms that regulate law-making identify the core identity of the legal order and its main characters. Kelsen opts for a procedural norm that is potentially intertwined with a conception of democracy. But given his commitment to methodological purity, he does not engage (in his legal theory, because his political philosophy could be read in quite different terms) with the corresponding social order. The question of the organisation of the social order does not register and it is not accounted for at the level of legal knowledge. In fact, the form of the law is objective because it is autonomous from the social order all the way down to its own foundational norm, and proper legal knowledge cannot be achieved if it is pursued by taking into account social relations. Notoriously, the lack of a coupling between the organisation of social relations and the basic norm creates tension in Kelsen's system as the latter seems, in the end, to require a certain degree of efficacy (for a reconstruction of the debate on Kelsen's conception of the basic norm, see Trivisonno, 2021). Yet, the idea of a fundamental norm cannot be dismissed easily if the analysis of the legal order emphasises normality over the extraordinary. Be that as it may, this is not the right place to discuss this aspect of Kelsen's rich and inspiring legal thought. The next section will introduce the founding modern tradition of thinking about the materiality of the legal order and highlight its limits.

2 Materialist Analysis of Law

It is not surprising that the first stream to have devoted proper and systematic attention to the materiality of the legal order has been nineteenth-century dialectic materialism. As the dominant framework, fundamentally liberal, for approaching the material dimension was to extoll the virtues of the separation between the social and the legal spheres, the reaction would focus on the way that relation should be conceived in altogether different terms. At the cost of simplifying a rather stratified and rich history, this is because of the different priorities of these two (liberalism and materialism) streams of thought. Both share the same analytical assumptions when it comes to the political economy emerging from the last quarter of the eighteenth century, that is, the centrality of division of labour and a labour-based conception of value, but they draw different lessons from that centrality. For liberal legal thinking, individual freedom is the northern star of the legal order and, for this reason, legal formalism seems to be an appropriate way to secure it. It is the separation between the social and the legal that makes it possible for the latter to operate as a guarantee of freedom and, most importantly, as the foundation for the rule of law and legal certainty. As is known, socialists and Marxists have engaged in different ways with the idea that the determinant of the form and the content of the law would be something not internal to the law itself but overdetermined by an undergirding set of social relations. Basically, the answer to the question of why the law has taken up a certain form would be looked for in the context of the political economy of the legal order. Certain social relations would function as determinants of legal facts. There is something important (and at the same time controversial) in this way of addressing the question and that is the fact that the modes and relations of production (over)determine the social and the legal order. A key difference with the formalist liberal approach concerns precisely the form of the law, which is not only, for the materialist, an expression of a claim (or a duty) but one of the forms taken up by social relations. As already noted, from a materialist perspective, a set of particular social relations is determinative of the legal order. These are relations of production and organise the political economy of a modern society. As is evident, such a conception is typical of modern legal orders with a high degree of specialisation and differentiation. Therefore, labour and its organisation becomes the engine of social and legal ordering as it is assumed, especially in a capitalist environment, that a social order can be constituted and reproduced only under certain conditions of productive organisation. Even if this is just a quick and simplified sketch of the materialist understanding of the social order, the difference from the political theories broached in the previous section should already be visible. The productive organisation of labour relations as a formative factor of social order cannot be subsumed easily under those three main approaches. Although labour can be understood as interest or as a sacrificial practice, and although its value can be reconstructed in a way that is potentially compatible with a conventional view of society, the actual unfolding of social organisation remains irreducible to those aspects. It is not only the fact that social organisation requires both differentiation and co-operation, hence it cannot easily be taken into account in schemes that aim at solving prisoner's-dilemma kinds of issue. In fact, central to Marx's materialist understanding of reality is the relation between man and nature: it is that relation that makes up the materiality of the social order. And it provides the objective ground of Marxist's materialism: understanding reality means grasping the fundamental components of the materiality relation. Ultimately, the latter is animated by an activity: *labour*. The relation between man and nature is mediated by this activity, which becomes the building block of societal formation when human beings organise it. It should also be added that the organisation of labour is a matter of normality rather than exceptional arrangement. By definition, harnessing labour to a productive organisation implies framing not only a sense of normality but, rather, a horizon within which that normality takes its shape. Producing is therefore a key component for the development of society and it requires the emergence of the legal order as well. Indeed, the organisation of production can operate properly – that is, be harnessed to value generation – only if it is normalised as an ordinary activity. Norms concerning labour organisation and division will eventually introduce a sense of normality. Nonetheless, a conflictual dimension is inherent in the division of labour, and the distribution of roles and functions that comes with it. As we shall see, according to this materialist version of social ordering, societal formation pivots around the struggles ignited by the principle of division of labour.

2.1 Marx's Conception of the Materiality of Law

The philosophy of Karl Marx is the obvious starting point for this way of looking at the materiality question. His unsystematic reflection on law provided the canvas for the future development of a materialist view of the legal order. His precious intuition was to place at the centre of the question of the materiality of social organisation the notion of productive labour, and the authority created for exercising 'commanding power' over it. Unfortunately, the lack of systematic reflection on the role of law in Marx's published works has paved the way to a rather reductionist way of thinking about the materiality of the legal order. It might be said that his conception of productive activities, while rightly based on labour as the fundamental social relation, develops at times as a monodimensional notion. Labour is indeed analysed in its industrial dimension and it is conceived as alienated labour,[6] whose appropriation is also deemed to be the centre of gravity of the fundamental relation between capital and labour itself. This conflictual relation is generative because it is a fundamental cleavage around which societal organisation develops. In a quite original way, certain writings by Marx imagine that it is even possible to track an autonomous conception of labour's existence (cf. Negri, 1984), which would make the establishment of labour relations a feature of society independent from the command of capital and with a capacity for self-organisation.

Be that as it may, the orthodox picture of law portrayed by Marx and many of his followers is premised on the distinction between base and suprastructure, that is, on the categorical difference between the structural organisation of economic relations and the other systems that are dependent, for their formation, on the former. The argument that law is a system that belongs to the

---

[6] In Marx's writings there is also space for a different view on labour: as not only a source of domination but also a potential way for self-realisation. This conception is especially visible in the pages of the *Grundrisse* dedicated to labour as sacrifice in Adam Smith: Marx, 1980, pp. 123–8.

suprastructure, ultimately determined by the material forces that operate in the economic base, was first developed by Marx in *The German Ideology*. On this understanding, the political economy is the *base* of every society, determining its shape and the form of its institutions. Law, as it is located among the systems of the suprastructure, is very much aligned to the base that conditions the mode of production. Its operation thus broadly reflects the necessities of the mode of production and its function is to sustain and regulate capitalist economic and social relations. It is essential to highlight that, under this description, law is not constitutive of economic and social relations. Its function is rather to enforce and protect already existing social relations. In short, under this description, *the materiality relation is one of monodirectional determination: the structure of social relations determines the form and the content of the legal order.*

Concerns over whether this kind of determinism can be avoided remain. An important example is represented by the *Preface to the Critique of Political Economy*, where, in one of the most discussed passages of his work, Marx notes in typically deterministic fashion that 'the mode of production of material life conditions the general process of social, political and intellectual life. It is not the consciousness of men that determines their existence, but their social existence that determines their consciousness' (Marx, 1996, p. 426). The organisation of the modes and relations of production drives historical development, and the law is a product of such development that is too often presented as a 'reflex' of the underlying dynamics of the process of production: 'At a certain stage of development, the material productive forces of society come into conflict with the existing relations of production or – this merely expresses the same thing in legal terms – with the property relations within the framework of which they have operated hitherto' (Marx, 1996, p. 426). This last quote has often been highlighted as proof of Marx's reductive view of the legal order, where property relations are seen as mere instantiations of an already constituted set of modes and relations of productions. According to this interpretation, other legal institutions (e.g., the family) are also seen as reflexes of underlying structures of production (i.e., modes and relations). *The German Ideology* is usually read as a representative text of this reductive view: in it, Marx attacks directly a certain way of understanding the law as the product of an act of pure will, an idea that he denounces as 'the legal illusion', and that makes him suspicious of purely positivist descriptions of law. Marx rejects altogether a conception of law that makes it the outcome of a purely autonomous political decision. And yet *The German Ideology* contains a clear and important distinction between two conceptions of the law, first as *will* and then as *power*. Marx's efforts are often directed at criticising the will-based conception of law by linking the law back to the concrete relations of power from which it emanates, and in the context of which even those who find themselves in an advantageous position cannot simply bend the law to impose their arbitrary will. The will of those empowered by the structure of social relations cannot but be conditioned by the 'real relations' which are the source of their power:

> The individuals who rule in these conditions – leaving aside the fact that their power must assume the form of the *state* – have to give their will, which is determined by these definite conditions, a universal expression as the will of the state, as law, an expression whose content is always determined by the relations of this class, as the civil and criminal law demonstrates in the clearest possible way. . . . [J]ust as the weight of their bodies does not depend on their idealistic will or on their arbitrary decision, so also the fact that they enforce their own will in the form of law, and at the same time to make it independent of the personal arbitrariness of each individual among them, does not depend on their idealistic will (Marx, 1976, p. 327)

This is an instantiation of Marx's concern as a materialist author to go beyond the phenomenal world in order to retrieve the logic of the principles that animate that world. In the third volume of *Capital*, this methodology is summarised in a context where the discussion focusses on the main pillars of modern political economy: 'But all science would be superfluous if the outward appearance and the essence of things directly coincided' (Marx, 1991b, p. 897). This statement sums up in an elegant way both how Marx addresses the relation between the material and the phenomenal (matter and appearance) and how he tries to overcome Hegel's idealist take on historical development. Though still a matter of intense debate among Marxists, this point might mark an essential difference between the two thinkers. While in Hegel history and the formation of its driving idea are impossible to separate, otherwise reality would be irrational, in Marx the relation comes across as more ambiguous. Within the perimeter of Marx's works, there is room to recover a *richer* conception of law without having to abandon the critique of political economy.

The best place, perhaps, to begin a reconstruction of Marx's materialist theory of law is an often neglected text: *The Critique of Hegel's Doctrine of the State* (printed in Marx, 1996, pp. 57–198). This is Marx's unfinished first manuscript, which appeared only later (in 1927) in the Soviet Union. Besides offering us Marx's most extensive account of his complex but decisive relation with Hegel, it also contains his most elaborated statement on the law, the role of property, the form of government and the state. The key idea that Marx extrapolates from Hegel is to be found in the productive effects of *negation*. The dialectic unfolding of history is indeed moved by the power of negation. But a key difference already emerges at this stage, one that turns Hegel's insight on the formation of consciousness on its head: negation is the constitutive act for the formation of subjectivity. Crucially, Marx will translate this intuition into the idea that history is made by and through class struggle, moved by a class that draws constitutively on the *negation* of its identity, role, and speaking position in the extant order. Of course, this type of negation is still dialectic because it does not entail sheer and intractable antagonism (of the type friend/enemy) but rather contains the seeds for its own overcoming. The centrality of class struggle implies that the formation of social organisation is deeply intertwined with processes of differentiation and, in the case of the relations of production, generative of domination.

For the legal theorist, the main challenge is to understand the place of law within the historical developments brought about by class struggle. The critique of Hegel's dialectic, applied to the philosophy of law, reveals two key aspects of Marx's thought, central to the materialist nature of his methodology. First is the rejection of Hegel's version of the dialectic method as prone to mystification on two levels. The first mystification (referred to by Marx as 'mystique of reason') is the equivalence established by Hegel between being and thought, the real and the rational. This equivalence entails a double inversion. On one level, being is reduced to thought and hence the concrete is denied autonomous reality. On another level, reason becomes an absolute and self-sufficient reality. In order to assume autonomous existence, the idea has to be embodied; it has to be carried into concrete existence. Such a move corresponds to inversion of the order and meaning between subject and predicate. Commenting on section 279 of Hegel's *Philosophy of Right*, Marx notes: 'Hegel makes the predicates, the objects, autonomous, but he does this by separating them from their real autonomy, *viz*, their subject. The real subject subsequently appears as a result whereas the correct approach would be to start with the real subject and then consider its objectification' (Marx, 1996, p. 78). Hegel's 'mystical' approach to reality fundamentally denies its material existence. The second major mystification concerns Hegel's idealised concept of the state. While, according to Hegel, the state is an achieved synthesis of ethics (*Sittlichkeit*) and morality beyond civil society, that is, a rational expression of the spirit, Marx (whose conception of the state remained notoriously underdeveloped) takes it to be a complex field whose formation and growth are intimately linked to the development of capitalism. Although later described as the political agent of the bourgeoisie, and despite the lack of a fully developed theory, Marx's concept of the state hints at its constitutive role in both allowing capitalism to flourish and serving as an internal limit to certain forms of accumulation (cf. Jessop, 2015).

In light of the previous remarks, it is not surprising that, unlike Hegel, Marx does not see law as necessarily rational. However, this judgement does not imply necessarily that the legal order ought to be classified as a suprastructural feature of the political economy (although this remains a viable interpretation) or as a tool that can be used in infinite ways according to the needs of capital. If the legal order resists such reductions, it is because its form does not lend itself easily to manipulation. Instead, there are important passages in Marx's oeuvre that allow us to imagine a more active, and at times even constitutive, role for the law. These passages, although not systematic, suggest that capitalist development is not dictated by a mechanical dialectic, or that law is properly understood to fall on the side of *structure* rather than *agency*. In other words, the political economy of capitalist societies evolves because its central engine is class struggle (Hunter, 2021). It is only by retrieving the central role of class struggle that it is possible to avoid a reductionist view of the legal order as a mere reflex of the political economy. To acknowledge its centrality is to acknowledge that all actors involved in the struggle can play an active or a reactive role. It is not necessarily capital that is 'in charge' of the development of the social order. Labour can impose constraints on capital as well, and force it to introduce innovation as a way to defuse or alleviate class struggle (Tronti, 2019).

An important example of the relative autonomy of law in shaping fundamental social relations can be found in *Capital*, in the chapter on legislation on the working day. Reconstruction of the struggle around labour time, for both young persons and children, is obviously a crucial theme in the exploitation (and the relation between productivity and surplus value) of the labour force. Marx connects legislation (a modern form of law) with class struggle in the most direct way: 'The establishment of a normal working day is therefore the product of a protracted and more or less concealed civil war between the capitalist class and the working class' (Marx, 1991a, p. 412). Hence, a precious lesson can be learnt: legislation is not inherently or monolithically a reflection of the interests of the owners of means of production as, unlike a 'pompous catalogue of the inalienable rights of man', it establishes the moment when the worker's time is their own and not for sale any longer (Marx, 1991a, p. 416). This chapter of *Capital* illustrates two important points. First, it clearly indicates that class struggle can be driven by labour's initiative and can shape legislation (but also lawmaking in general) in a way that is not overdetermined by capital's interests. Second, it shows that law (in this case, in the form of legislation) is not exclusively an instrument in the hands of owners of means of production for the moulding of labour relations in favour of their own interests. Law is embedded in class struggle and whether it can be bent or used in different ways remains a question of internal constraints (meaning: internal to the form of the law) and external social context (meaning: economic incentives and culture).

The notion of materiality in Marx's thought on the legal order is not only visible in these scattered remarks found in the *Grundrisse* and in *Capital*. There is another interesting, yet underexplored way of looking at the emergence of the legal order and its link with social relations that can be found by looking at a set of observations made by Carl Schmitt on Marx's political philosophy. As is known, in the last phase of his intellectual trajectory, the German jurist Schmitt became more attentive to legal institutionalism and the notion of the concrete order (Croce and Salvatore, 2022). The concept of *nomos* became central to his legal thinking; every legal order, according to Schmitt, is formed by its *nomos*. This entails a unity of order and orientation (Schmitt, 2006, p. 42), and the formation of the *nomos* is concomitant with the emergence of the social order. A *nomos* provides both the measure of the relations that is supposed to organise and guide and, at the same time, the form of those relations. In a couple of short articles published (in English) as the appendix of the *Nomos of the Earth*, Schmitt insisted that the formation of a legal order must follow a precise series of phases that are already 'announced' by the etymology of the word *nomos*: appropriation, distribution, production. The origin of the order is always a taking (Lindahl, 2019, p. 171) and for this reason, in the beginning, 'there was no basic norm, but a basic appropriation' (Schmitt, 2006, p. 345). For Schmitt, it is important that lawyers recognise the legal relevance of this first moment as it is jurisgenerative. However, he thought that the majority of legal and political theories were mistakenly focussed on the wrong order of phases. Both liberals and socialists, according to Schmitt, would imagine that distribution and redistribution constitute the formative phase of every legal and social order. Socialists and communists would also tend to overemphasise the phase of production as a formative moment. When it comes to Marx, Schmitt concedes that while the most pressing concern is for production, there is also some attention paid to the moment of appropriation because of the dictatorship of the proletariat. According to Schmitt, in the Marxian account the legal order is reduced to a reflex of the economic structure because it misses the original formation of the order as concrete order. More specifically, Schmitt believes that Marx does not recognise openly that the inception of the order is given by an appropriation. Marx confused the relation of cause and effect between appropriation and production because of the emphasis on production and distribution. In other words, if Schmitt's critique is correct, then Marx's idea of the materiality of the legal order ought to be put into question. In fact, according to this reconstruction, Marx would miss the thematisation of the key original and formative moment of land-grabbing, which would be, according to Schmitt, already loaded with the political will of forming a legal order with specific objectives. Hans Lindahl has captured the core function of this moment of appropriation by describing it anew as a retaking:

> [A]n act of appropriation, if it is not to spin in empty air, must be a novel ordering of economic and distributive processes that appear retroactively, through the appropriation, as *already* having a certain order or unity. Such an appropriation seems to do no more than *re*appropriate or *re*take the product- ive and distributive order in a way that makes possible the self-assertion of a collective (Lindahl, 2019, p. 294).

But, as Schmitt himself recognises, Marx is aware of the important role of the original appropriation. First, a proper reading of the last chapters of *Capital* volume 1 shows that the notion of primitive accumulation entails an original appropriation as well. Marx develops his analysis in historical mode, but from these chapters a clear view of the origins of a legal order can be retrieved. The original appropriation sets up the capitalist modern legal order by opening up a first channel of accumulation of wealth. While Marx does not pause to consider the role of law in that first phase of construction of capitalist legal orders, it is quite evident that his reconstruction implies at least two important points. The violence entailed by the act of dispossessing the inhabitants of the land or appropriating commons is a core feature of the emerging legal order. In chapter 28 of volume 1, he describes the creation of the wage labourer through the workings of English legislation. Even more importantly, when Marx affirms that primitive accumulation is the outcome of the capitalist mode of production, he does not mean that one is the effect and the other the cause. In another chapter of the last part of *Capital* volume 1 (chapter 26), Marx states clearly that primitive accumulation 'is not the result of the capitalist mode of production but its point of departure' (Marx, 1991a, p. 876). Not only is primitive accumu- lation the precondition for developing a certain mode of production but the philosophy behind such production is already inscribed in the logic of primitive accumulation, and this is so clear to Marx that he resorts to a theological metaphor to explain it: 'this primitive accumulation plays approximately the same role in political economy as original sin does in theology' (Marx, 1991a). The original appropriation, which is functionally equivalent to Schmitt's taking, is therefore included in the development of the legal order. Not only is it a precondition for the emergence of a certain type of legal order but it carries its own principles into the legal order in the following phases. A second point is less evident as it is not developed fully by the author of *Capital*. As Schmitt himself admits, Marx advocates a retaking as the political path towards social transformation. The 'expropriation of the expropriators' is a short formula that captures what Marx believed to be the right way to overcome a capitalist social order. Obviously, this implies an appropriation of the means of production on a huge scale. For Schmitt, this is confirmation that Marx has to come to terms with the unavoidable moment of appropriation and that this is far from being fully determined by modes and relations of production. From Schmitt's perspective, this is better apprehended as the political moment in Marx's philosophy.

Overall, despite his unsystematic contribution, Marx offers an important insight into the materiality of the legal order. According to him, every mode and set of relations of production is shaped, though not exclusively, by legally characterised ways of appropriating. One can find references to the constitutive role of property as a fundamental legal relation scattered throughout his many works. Marx alludes to the fact that the *mode of appropriation* and the *mode of production* are deeply intertwined from the outset. But, crucially, the mode of appropriation revolves around a particular institutional figure of property. Marx does not question the role of personal private property, that is, a form of property that entails ownership of personal belongings. What is crucial for creation of a capitalist mode of production is appropriation of the means of production and, emphatically, the type of property 'which rests on the exploitation of alien, but formally free labour' (Marx, 1991bb, p. 928). In other words, the formation of a capitalist legal order cannot be disconnected meaningfully from appropriation of the surplus value generated by labour. But, in order to appropriate surplus value, it is necessary to set up a legal system that makes it possible to force people into looking for employment and turns labour into an exchangeable commodity (i.e., into labour force). In light of these remarks, the materiality relation within a capitalist organisation can be redescribed as the articulation of a property relation that shapes the social order across the divide between capital and labour under the imperative of valorisation. Accordingly, the legal order is not applied to this already formed societal order; it is inherent in the ability to organise capitalist relations from their inception.

2.2 A Reductionist Materialism

If Marx offered some underexplored entry points to the question of the materiality relation, other nineteenth-century materialists foreclosed the possibility of a reconstruction that would not fall prey to a version of vulgar materialism. In this way, they discredited the analytical quality of materialist legal analysis.

A classic example of this reductionist approach is the work of Ferdinand Lassalle, whose understanding of the reality of a constitutional order is rather telling of the ideology-critique approach to the question of materiality. Lassalle introduced a distinction between the 'real constitution' – societal organisation – and the written constitution (sometimes pejoratively defined as a 'piece of paper') and postulated that the former would completely condition the latter (for a similar analysis, see Engels' comments on the English Constitution). More specifically, Lassalle seems to imply an equivalence between the constitutional text and norms, but he denies that they are part of social reality. To the question 'what is the nature of the constitution?', Lassalle replied with the following definition: 'a constitution is the fundamental law proclaimed in a country which disciplines the organization of public rights in that nation' (Lassalle, 1942, n.p.). This is because, fundamentally, Lassalle thought that 'constitutional questions are not primordially legal questions, but a matter of relations of force' (Lassalle, 1942, n.p.). By stating that the constitution is the fundamental law of the country, Lassalle assumed that it has higher value than ordinary law and that it has its own grounding, so that 'it must be none other than what it is. Its basis will not permit it to be otherwise' (Lassalle, 1942, n.p.). The basis of the legal order has to be found 'always and exclusively in the real effective relations among social forces in a given society' (Lassalle, 1942, n.p.). What remains unclear is whether the real constitution, that is, the organisation of the dominant forces within a society, is also a juridical constitution or only a deeply entrenched state of affairs. Lassalle's imperativist conception of law makes the nature of the real constitution ambiguous and, accordingly, the same can be said of its relation with the written constitution. It is not entirely clear how the formal constitution becomes only a cover for the social organisation of production. In fact, it seems that the real constitution becomes law only when codified in written form and with the introduction of explicit sanctions: 'these actual relations of force are put down on paper, are given written form, and after they have been thus put down, they are no longer simply actual relations of force but have now become *laws*, judicial institutions, and whoever opposes them is punished' (Lassalle, 1942, n.p.). Under this description, the formal constitution represents the juridification of the 'real' relations of power or, in the most trivial sense, it is just the registration or codification of the real constitution. Lassalle is adamant in stating that the formal constitution is stable and lasting 'only when it corresponds . . . to the real constitution, that is, to the real relations among social forces' (Lassalle, 1942, n.p.). Otherwise, it is just a sham constitution. Be that as it may, according to Lassalle the relation between materiality and the letter of the constitution is one of mismatch between the former and the latter. In the cases where the two orders overlap, one becomes basically the legal mirror of the other. When there is a distance between the material and the written constitution, the latter is simply the ideological mask covering the underlying relationships of power or, at best, providing a veneer of legitimacy. In other words, Lassalle maintains that the social order of production is already shaped pre-politically and pre-constitutionally. At best, the formal constitution operates as part of the justificatory ideological apparatus of the undergirding dominant social forces. The limit of such a rigid materialist take is that it reduces the legal order to an effect of other social processes, that is, the legal order remains in an external relation to social organisation. Relations of production are rightly put at the centre of the analysis, but how those relations came to take up those *modes* and *forms* of production is never thematised. Representing the relation of materiality in this way is not conducive to an accurate understanding as the hegemony of the dominant forces is presented as not having any normative underpinning and one is left wondering how those political and economic powers have been able to mould the social order. Perhaps the most troubling aspect of this reductionist materialism concerns the epistemic level. Both Marx and Lassalle indulge at length the idea that there is an apparent reality and a deeper one, not immediately visible, but structurally essential. The task for the observer who wants to address the materiality question is to avoid the superficial level of the phenomena and retrieve the undergirding structural reality, the one that really matters.

Perhaps, the lack of nuances in that materialist approach is dictated by the historical context and the type of legal order that someone like Lassalle was directly observing. In the twentieth century, aided by some dramatic changes in the institutional context of the likes of the expansion of the franchise and the growth of many intermediary bodies, several materialist authors realised that reductionism is not a promising avenue and tried to expound the thesis of the relative autonomy of other systems vis-à-vis economic relations of production. But, for example, in 1905 Lenin was still defending a reductive version of materialism in *Materialism and Empiriocriticism* (Lenin, 2002, ch. V), where the idea that reality is made of matter and can be objectively apprehended is resolutely supported. This type of realism provides the structure of natural and, also, social reality. Indeed, Lenin condemns any attempt at introducing other aspects beyond this rather crude materialism.[7] The risk, he believes, is to fall

---

[7] Lenin's main targets are Mach and Alexander Bogdanov. The latter is a relatively unknown figure in the Western world, although his metaphysics and his theory of organisation are of great originality. Unfortunately, Bogdanov did not write on law, but put forward a science of organisation, known as 'tektology', which contains intuitions later developed, without direct influence, by legal institutionalists and systems theory (Bogdanov, 2022). From the living organism to social groups, what makes up reality is the organisation of the relations among elements. Natural life (from the cell to more complex organism) is a web of relations; in parallel, social life is the organisation of collective labour. Bogdanov understood the collective as antecedent to the individual and included intellectual labour among the collective processes of social organisation. Crucially, Bogdanov was convinced that the fundamental aspect of the capitalist mode of production was not the private property of the means of production but the organisation of labour. Bogdanov believed that private ownership was detrimental for the needs of society, but was equally convinced that state property would have produced the same negative effects because even a change in the status of property would not have revolutionised how production was

back into a form of idealism (which, for him, is the form of the bourgeois state). Lenin was not followed by the vast majority of European Marxists, most of whom devoted their efforts to presenting a more nuanced picture of the relations among different systems. From Rosa Luxembourg to Antonio Gramsci and Georg Lukács, many Marxist authors have attempted to go beyond the rigid distinction between the base and the suprastructure. But the vast majority of these authors have not engaged directly with the link between societal formation and the legal order. Another stream of thought, legal institutionalism, focusses its investigations on that node, and for this reason the next section is entirely devoted to it.

3 Legal Institutionalism

Legal institutionalism is a stream of legal theory that gained traction in the inter-war period. The social and intellectual context that gave birth to legal institutionalism cannot be ignored and it explains many of the concerns at the forefront of legal institutionalists' works. On one hand, the crisis of the liberal state under the pressure of demands for inclusion put forward by the masses and the tragedy of World War I provided a context where a purely formalist understanding of the law would come across as untenable, or largely inaccurate. On the other hand, the rise and consolidation of sociology with its attention on society as an object of study pushed legal theorists to focus their attention on the relation between societal formation and the legal order. Coupled to the rise of sociology was the creation of a new field, social law, which found in legal institutionalism an obvious theoretical ally. The end of the overlapping between the social basis of the legal order and its formal organisation showed the limits of a liberal and neutral approach to legal theory. The multiplication of social groups, striving for legal and political recognition, set the stage for an intense political conflict with state institutions. Societal formation is conceived not as a consequence of co-ordination of individuals' actions but as an incessant mitosis of associations. Gunther Teubner has captured this peculiar trait of legal institutionalism, in its relation with the proliferation of social forces, in the following terms: 'Institutionalist theories and, in particular, the new discipline of sociology ... came up with more complex self-description of society' (Teubner, 2012, p. 21).

One can think of legal institutionalism as a constellation whose main planets revolve around the same focus, but they all maintain their own distinct

---

organised. What was necessary, according to him, was a more accurate understanding of the monist character of reality and, accordingly, a different way of organising labour activities so as to overcome the capitalist division of labour.

trajectory. When observing this constellation from a wider perspective, it is possible to detect some common themes that set its countours. The first is methodological and possibly the most important for understanding the materiality of law. Unlike the reductionist streak of the materialist view, legal institutionalists begin by assuming that there is an *internal* connection, rather than a relation of supervenience,[8] between societal formation and legal ordering. Law is seen as one of the techniques for shaping social relations, but its development is also driven by the articulation of social relations. Institutionalists do not deny that the organisation of the social order is at stake, but they do not understand it as dictated exclusively by an economic vector. They also do not share liberal assumptions about that relation. Unlike classic liberal legal thought, the legal order is not grafted onto an already existing social system for the purpose of protecting individual freedom. According to the institutionalists, societal formation is a complex process that proceeds through a variety of means and languages of which the legal order is one of the most relevant. For this reason, it is impossible to understand the legal order without seeing it as part of society's partial self-description. For the institutionalists, society is not a self-transparent object of study. Hence, in order to be described and understood, it has to be accessed from specific angles. It is not surprising, then, that this internal relationship between societal formation and legal ordering is often one of *integration*. The process of legal ordering is an expansive process of subsuming into itself different social and cultural dimensions. Also, the internal connection between legal ordering and social relations turns the classic distinction between the extraordinary and normality upside down. The main interest for legal institutionalists is how legal ordering builds and maintains patterns of normality. There is nothing outside society or the legal order that sets social relations into motion. Reversing the famous sentence by Schmitt, normality reveals the function of the emergency. It is not the emergency that energises the legal order because ordering is an activity whose finality is one of building normality and the ordinary. In other words, the point of ordering is to define and create normality and, in an integrative logic, all emergencies and extraordinary activities are oriented towards protection of that normality.

Furthermore, according to legal institutionalists, it is wrong to look at social relations without putting on the lenses of juridical science. The jurist is not supposed to turn into a sociologist, but it has to recognise the juridical traces present in social organisation and it has to favour, with its expertise, the process

---

[8] A relation of supervenience obtains when no two things (A and B) can differ with respect to their *A*-properties without also differing with respect to their *B*-properties.

of amalgamation between social spheres and legal ordering. In that respect, although there are some overlaps, legal institutionalism remains distinct from the later iterations of socio-legal studies.

A second important common trait concerns the role of institutions. These are the building blocks of the legal order's materiality. The formation of institutions is the matter which makes up the materiality of the legal order precisely because institutions are the element of integration between organised social relations and the legal order. The content of institutions is a cluster of norms organised around a directive idea, a goal, an orientation, ethical principles or fundamental political aims. In a nutshell, norms and organisation are the constitutive elements of the institution. As is evident, this notion of the institution is supposed to consolidate the interweaving of social relations and the legal order.

A third important common trait is given by the focus on the idea of the legal order, which is, again, tied to exploration of the materiality of law. The idea of the legal order is used by legal institutionalists as opposed or alternative to the idea of the legal system. This is a conventional distinction in the sense that not all linguistic uses of legal system are alternative to the notion of the legal order. Actually, it is perfectly legitimate to understand the idea of a system of rules as a way to make sense of the legal order (Lindahl, 2019, pp. 132–5). The idea of the legal order does not presuppose necessarily a plan or a project (see the difference in the conception expanded by Shapiro, 2011), although it might contain it, but it is marked by an orientation or teleological element. To borrow a term from grammar studies, legal ordering is a telic activity. Its performative capacity is proportionate to its capacity to move towards certain aims. Again, this idea of the legal order remains in sharp contrast with the neutral idea of the legal system as a hierarchy of norms. There might be a norm of closure, but for epistemic rather than teleological reasons. As we shall see, the hierarchy of norms is not evacuated from the legal order; it is organised on the basis of the telic elements that orient the legal order. And, crucially, the telic dimension of ordering is legally relevant. It does not remain external to legal knowledge.

Yet, all three of these themes have been expounded in interesting ways by different authors. Think, for example, about the monism of legal orders: some institutionalists have implied that legal orders require a hierarchy of institutions under the umbrella of an encompassing order, while others have put forward a claim in support of the irreducible plurality of legal orders. The remainder of this section will deal with some selected figures of classic legal institutionalism. Because the constellation of thinkers is too varied to be fully accounted for in this Element, the following is aimed at providing an idea of the richness and the nuances of this constellation by separating it into two approaches: one is more attentive to the capacity for organising social relations (generative institutionalism) while the other considers the question of materiality to be a matter of how integration into society is realised by legal institutions (integrative institutionalism).

3.1 Generative Institutionalism

Maurice Hauriou is rightly considered a founding father of the legal institutionalist stream. His approach was developed in reaction against the two most influential perspectives in the French debate of the time: the objectivist conception of law expounded by Léon Duguit and the sociology of Émile Durkheim. The main objective of Hauriou's theory is to provide an anti-voluntaristic, objective reconstruction of the legal order on the basis of its relation with social groups and projects that strive to achieve a given aim. Neither the social contract nor the rule of law can provide a real basis for the legal order. The solution to the dichotomy between subjectivist and objectivist theories of law is the institution. The crucial import of Hauriou's position is that positive rules are created by institutions, but the opposite is not true (Hauriou, 1970, p. 123). Institutions are the sources of law, but their nature is not exhausted by their normative framework because they also have a vital spiritual dimension. Hence, positive rules are what today could be defined as regulative rules. Positive law, according to Hauriou, operates only in the modality of posing limits and constraints. The creative and generative dimension of the legal order is at a different level: an idealistic pull coming from objective ideas that constitute and lead the institution.

According to how the idea is internalised by the institution, there can be two types of institution: 'person-institution' (*institution*) and 'object-institution' (*chose institution*). Unfortunately, object-institutions are treated only marginally by Hauriou, and they are characterised by the lack of subjectivation of the guiding idea. In light of the contemporary concern for nature and non-human subjects, it is a pity that such an intuition has not been developed further. Person-institutions represent the most basic element of the legal order and they are those that really interest Hauriou. The definition of institution contains three constitutive elements: 'An institution is an idea of a work or enterprise that is realized and endures juridically in a social context; for the realization of this idea, an organized power equips it with organs; on the other hand, among the members of the social group interested in the realization of the idea, manifestations of communion occur and are directed by the organs of the power and regulated by procedures' (Hauriou, 1970, p. 99). In short, one can detect three defining tenets of an institution: (1) its existence is directed by and towards an ordering idea (*idée directrice*); (2) there is an organisation that endows the institution with proper power and organs for realising the idea; and (3) there are forms of solidarity that hold the institution together and provide the support for its endurance. It should be made clear that the ordering idea does not serve a teleological function or play the role of a fundamental objective of a social group. While all three elements are essential, the distinctive one (the one that gives to the institution its own specific identity) is the driving or ordering idea. This might be generated by certain fundamental aims, but in time it allows what is at the beginning only psychological intention to be transferred into social reality. In the long term, the idea transcends the original aims and acquires its own distinctive logic. Moreover, the directive idea has a creative and reflexive nature, and it can rethink or transform the original aims of the social group (La Torre, 2010, p. 147).

The temporal extension of the ordering idea is key for making it autonomous and independent of the connected fundamental political objectives. At the same time, in order to become autonomous, the driving idea needs to gather enough and constant consensus from the members of the institution. This consensus is not a truly collective will: 'it is individuals who are moved by their contact with a common idea and who, by a phenomenon of interpsychology, become aware of their common emotion. The centre of this movement is the idea that is refracted into similar concepts in thousands of minds and that stirs these minds into action' (Hauriou, 1970, p. 107).

The three elements correspond to the end result of the constituent process of formation of the institution itself. Indeed, the process can be divided into three phases: first, *introjection* of the driving idea; second, *incorporation* of the idea into an organised power; and, finally, the moment of *specification*, in which 'the group members are absorbed in the idea of the work, the organs are absorbed in a power of realization, the manifestations of communion are psychical manifestations' (Hauriou, 1970, p. 101).

In the end, though, it seems that Hauriou adheres to the tradition of *droit politique* (cf. Loughlin, 2017) and assumes that the organisation of society, under conditions of modernity, can be achieved only by the macro-institution of the state. This becomes evident when he requires that, for an institution to be properly organised, a set of standards have to be met. These standards clearly echo constitutive elements of the modern state. The definition of the condition of durability speaks eloquently about the statist background of Hauriou's institutionalist thinking: 'A social organisation becomes durable, that is, able to conserve its specific form despite the continual renewal of the human matter it contains, when it is instituted, that is, when (1) the directing idea that is in it from the moment of its foundation has succeeded in subordinating to itself the governmental power, owing to balances of organs and of power, and (2) the system of ideas and balances has been ratified in its form by the consent of the members of the institution and of the social milieu as well' (Hauriou, 1970, p. 135). In other words, it is only when the guiding idea takes control of the structure of the separation of powers and animates political representation that a proper 'person-institution' comes alive and is objectified in social reality. These requirements limit social relations' capacity for creating institutions as only a certain scale and availability of power can stabilise such institutions.

Hauriou's institutionalism had the merit of having introduced an objectivist conception of the institution and this represents a first important step towards a more accurate and non-reductionist account of the relation between social formation and legal ordering. Yet, in the end he develops his intuition in the direction of a state-centric legal theory whose capacity for explaining autonomous social organisation is impaired by its reliance on traditional doctrines of *droit politique*. The materiality of the legal order is touched upon, but it is not fully thematised. Be that as it may, Hauriou's conception of the institution will prove seminal for other legal institutionalists.

Together with Hauriou, Romano is justly deemed to be a founding father of legal institutionalism. The dominance of the social dimension of the legal order in his work is captured by the famous Latin sentence *ubi societas, ibi ius*, which Romano refers to for showing the inextricable relationship between social reality and legal ordering. Despite the fact that he was educated under the wings of the Italian dean of public law studies Vittorio Emanuele Orlando, known for his method of systematic constitutional analysis revolving around the idea of the state-person, Romano understood already at the beginning of the twentieth century the importance of thinking of the legal order in deep connection with social needs and interests. In his view, the rise of trade unions, political parties, and other intermediate bodies represented a proper challenge not only for the classic methodology of public law but for the theory of law altogether. For this reason, his version of legal institutionalism was the first to take seriously the connection between societal formation and legal ordering. This is obtained by assuming as its building block the concept of institution and then asserting a striking equation: institutions are legal orders. In other words, institutions are not the sources of law; they are in themselves legal orders.

Romano's starting point is the opposite of liberal legal theory and it is steeped in concrete-order thinking: not freedom but *necessity* lies at the origin of legal orders. When looking for the original formation of institutions, Romano looks for the legal apprehension of social needs. The origin of the legal order is not constituent power, a creative force that can mould social relations in a way that expresses the highest degree of political freedom. Instead, one has to look at a passive aspect, necessity, which is 'the primary source of law, that is, of that law that emerges immediately and directly from social forces in a categorical, explicit and firm way . . . Necessity understood in this way is not the presupposition of a *regula iuris*, but it is *law in itself* . . .; the legislator cannot but recognise it and validate it' (Romano, 2019, pp. 142–3). Note that the work of all officials (not only judges but legislators and administrators as well) is first of all to recognise what is already there, as a matter of law, because of the state of necessity. Compared to the state-based institutionalism of Hauriou, we are clearly in a different territory. Necessity is law without the need of further institutional mediation, except for the jurist who is called to name it. There is a dominant factual component about necessity that brings Romano to claim that a state or government exists de facto. Yet, the core intuition behind his idea of the legal order is that of *ius involontarium*. Every legal order rests on an involuntary element. The consequences for the nature of legal order are remarkable: 'every legal order, apprehended in its comprehensive, but also critical dimension for understanding its nature, is revealed not as a complex of norms (which are actually a production and a derivation), but a social entity, with its own organisation' (Romano, 2019, p. 221). Only on the basis of a non-voluntary ordering can a voluntary one develop, though, intriguingly, it can never really efface the traces of the non-voluntary beginning. It is problematic to portray necessity as an objective state of things, but this is not the place for developing a criticism of the notion. What is interesting to note for the purpose of this Element is how necessity is used by Romano for connecting societal organisation and legal ordering. Necessity provides the entry point for articulating the materiality of the legal order. *Intrinsic* to the formation of a social entity, there is indeed a juridical dimension. The key idea is the one of *organisation*, which then leads to the formation of the institution. The creation of an entity entails an organised scheme and law is the technique that allows the shaping of that scheme into form. For this reason, the concept of law 'must be traced back to the concept of society' and 'must encompass the idea of social order' (Romano, 2019, p. 12).

Yet, not every social relation has to be understood in terms of an organisation. What then makes an organisation part not only of a social but also of a legal order? In order to answer this question, it is necessary to introduce Romano's conception of institution. Organisation is the key feature for defining what an institution is. In fact, an institution is the original and essential manifestation of law and it cannot be reduced to a mere aggregation of norms. While norms are necessary, they are not constitutive of the legal order. The generation of the latter can be discerned only by understanding social organisation. However, the definition of social organisation given by Romano comes in negative terms: 'organization, as I understand it here, is by no means a norm or a complex of norms; either because . . . it can be anterior to the norm; or because, when it is posterior to it and is linked with it, it is evidently a phenomenon that occurs as an effect of their enforcement, and thus it is not a norm' (Romano, 2019, p. 25). One can only speculate as to whether that organisation contains an immanent set of principles or a measure of order whose nature cannot be fully grasped by reference to regulative or constitutive rules. Crucially, but problematically at the same time, this view entails that organisation comes before norms. For this reason, it is necessary to delve further into the essential features of the concept of institution to grasp the work done by the ordering idea of organisation. For an institution to materialise, there have to be four distinctive aspects: (1) the entity has to possess an objective and concrete existence, which, even when immaterial, must be visible; (2) the entity must be a manifestation of the social nature of human beings; (3) it must possess its own individuality, that is, it must have a recognisable, distinct existence (but this does not mean that it cannot be related to other institutions: in fact, complex institutions are institution of institutions); and (4) the institution should be a firm and permanent unity that lasts in time (Romano, 2017, p. 19). In the economy of this definition, norms are necessary features, but they are not sufficient to be constitutive of the institution as they do not define its identity. Accordingly, 'the law cannot just be the norm established by the social organisation . . .[;] if it is true that the legal character of the latter is conferred by the social power that issues it, or at least sanctions it, it follows that this character must be already present in the institution, which could not assign such a legal character to the norm if it did not have it in itself' (Romano, 2017, p. 25). In fact, Romano is convinced that an institution can see all its norms changed and still remain identical to itself. This quality is related to the structural and objective nature of the institution. The institution is objective because it enjoys an 'effective, concrete and objective existence' (Romano, 2017, p. 32). Legal relationships take up their role only when they are inscribed into a structure, hence the law cannot be identified with them because the legal order 'is prior to them, in the sense that it consists in an organization or structure that is required in order for relationships – if and when they develop in its orbit – to be qualified as legal' (Romano, 2017, p. 67). At this point we can properly grasp how the internal relation between social and legal order is imagined by Romano: 'in order for an institution to arise, the existence of persons connected to each other through simple relationships is not enough as there must be a closer and more organic bond. The formation of a social super-structure is required upon which not only their distinct relationships, but also their own generic position depends [*sic*]' (Romano, 2017, p. 32). Legal relationships acquire their relevance only against the background of a permanent structure of organisation that distributes roles to agents and is designed to pursue one or more aims. The example provided by Romano is telling. Marriage is more than the legal relationship between two physical persons; it takes up its proper legal meaning only if understood in the legal terms of the institution of the family. This is because the organisation of the family as an institution distributes roles to its members, divides rights and duties among them, and manages their legal relationships. The social reality of marriage is a performative creation of the legal language. Hence, the essence of the law is not command. Rather, for Romano law is defined by its specific operations designed to establish a set of positions, powers, and authorities.[9]

Finally, it should be added that Romano is methodologically committed to the juristic method of knowledge (Itzcovich, 2020). The study of the concrete social entity that is the institution shall be conducted 'not from the point of view of the material forces that produce and sustain it, nor in relation to the environment where it develops and lives as a phenomenon intertwined with others, nor with regard to cause-effect relationships that affect it, and therefore, not sociologically, but in itself and for itself' (Itzcovich, 2020, p. 47). Jurists do play a fundamental role in reconstructing the materiality of the legal order. They do not have to look for causal relations between social groups and legal ordering. Rather, their work is to observe social reality by framing it in a legal manner. As has been rightly noted, Romano's approach to legal knowledge is more a practice of observation of social reality carried out with a technical language and categories of its own (Croce, 2018, p. 4). Social reality then becomes visible and objective through different mediums and the legal order is one of them. This means that the job of legal science is to determine the forms and the contents of the legal lexicon *from within* to account for the reality that surrounds the law. With Kelsen, Romano considers that legal knowledge ought to be a pure science. However, more explicitly than Kelsen would be ready to admit, it is an instrumental type of knowledge as it aims at ordering and stabilising society. While affirming the self-enclosed autonomy of legal knowledge, Romano's jurist is also playing a key function for societal ordering.

The wit and the depth of Romano's take on legal ordering are undeniable. Yet, despite the recognition of social conflict and differentiation as the drivers of legal ordering, it seems that social reflexivity is left largely unexplored by him. In particular, the analytical development of the idea of organisation as the core component of institutions seems to be detached from any form of reflexivity because Romano does not consider explicitly the level of secondary rules. Later, H. L. A. Hart (1994) will capture more clearly that move by introducing

---

[9] Romano (2017) imagines that there is something more to an institution than the aggregation of its parts. The theme of the relation between the whole and its parts reappears constantly in legal institutionalist scholarship, but for reasons of space cannot be addressed here.

secondary rules, that is, rules about rules. Romano's firm assertion that there is something more about organisation than a collection of norms excludes prima facie that reflexivity is expressed in terms of norms applied to norms. Yet, given the fact that the function of organisation is defined as a distribution of roles and positions, one is left wondering whether that distribution could be understood as a secondary level of norms.

A second intriguing variation of this kind of generative legal institutionalism comes from the work of Karl Llewellyn. Although he is known as one of the founders of legal realism, his work contains clear echoes of institutional thinking and does not revolve exclusively around judicial reasoning. In a way often resonant with Romano's institutionalism, Llewellyn has offered what has been called a 'thin functionalist' (Twining, 2009, p. 109) version of institutionalism. The thinness of the position lies in the fact that it does not presuppose law as the only tool for creating and maintaining social order and, moreover, it maintains that law might play other roles beyond ordering.

The starting point of Llewellyn's social theory of law is also reminiscent of Romano's, as it takes its move from the recognition that certain social needs must be met for a social group to form, stabilise, and pursue its purposes. In fact, it is unfair to reduce Llewellyn's legal theory to a short *ultra*-realist passage usually quoted from the *Bramble Bush*: 'what these officials do about disputes is, to my mind, the law itself' (Llewellyn, 2008, p. 3). A reading of some of Llewellyn's most influential works shows that he was advocating a wider way of studying and understanding law. In the economy of the analysis conducted in this Element, his theory of the law-jobs is of particular relevance for showing its functionalist underpinning. The jobs (i.e., social needs to be met) are classified by Llewellyn into six categories (but in some versions of his work they are five) and they are supposed to be necessary for all organised social groups. These are needs that a social group must address in its social development. Yet, the thin functionalism is indeed a consequence of the admission that law might not be the exclusive social device able to perform these tasks. It is worth listing all 'the jobs': (i) conflict resolution in order to discourage unlawful behaviours and to bring the relations of the disputants back into balance; (ii) preventive channelling of conduct and expectations; (iii) preventive channelling in order to adapt to change; (iv) allocation of authority and procedures for authoritative decision-making; (v) provision of direction (orientation) for the group; (vi) juristic method (Llewellyn, 1940). This is where institutions enter the stage. They are supposed to be the units that perform the so-called law-jobs. It should be added that listed ones are the essential law-jobs (meaning, without which there would not be an order), but there could be others as well. Hence, the definition of institution provided expressly by Llewellyn revolves around a cluster of law-jobs and comes with a functionalist undertone: 'An institution is in first instance organized activity built around the doing of a job or a cluster of jobs. A craft is a minor institution. A *major* institution differs in that its job-cluster is fundamental to the continuance of the society (or group)' (quoted by Twining, 2012, p. 177). In a recognisable institutionalist mode, Llewellyn distinguishes between essential and derivative institutions. Essential institutions are those that make up the material dimension of the legal order as they are fundamental for the maintenance of key social relations. Yet, the institution is not only a wholly functionalist creature as it requires ideals as well. In other words, an institution, in particular when it has to deal with a cluster of fundamental jobs for the existence of a social group, also maintains an intimate link with the purpose or point of the relevant social practices.

As it is for Romano, one of Llewellyn's main concerns is to account for the relation between societal formation and legal ordering by recognising patterns of legal pluralism. At the same time, he does not want to succumb to a form of panlegalism. As already said, law is not always the only way to address social needs. For this reason, he wants also to identify what distinguishes an institution from mere cultural regularities or etiquette. The institution contains a distribution of roles and positions that is not necessary for cultural regularities or etiquette. One of his most representative examples is a small institution like the family. Its members might have some traits or features in common; for example, they might be living together or they might be related by blood. Yet, once observed in its daily practice, it becomes evident that the component of the family performs different activities despite these common factors. But the patterns of behaviour are intertwined, forming a whole that 'we choose to call "a family", and which is more than and different from the constituent parts' (Llewellyn, 1934, p. 18). The same applies to the factory and, as an institution of institutions, to the corporation. We can see here the same motif found in Romano: organisation of a social group through distribution of roles and positions, and consolidation of different but interlocked behavioural patterns are the essential distinctive traits of the institution: 'it is the unlikeness plus the complementary crossplay of the organized ways which is the most convenient criterion for marking-off an institution from a mere "way" of simple culture-trait' (Llewellyn, 1934, p. 19). Moreover, institutions can be assembled in order to produce more complex and refined institutions.

However, unlike Romano, Llewellyn advocates a juristic method that is open to the social sciences. The focus of attention of the juristic method should be behaviour: 'not rules of law, nor norms, nor yet imperatives, *save as* these flow from, or are reflected in, or operate upon, behavior' (Llewellyn, 1941, p. 6).

Hence, the juristic method advocated by Llewellyn is more expansive than Romano's: it includes lawyers' traditional skills, but it encompasses all the ways of getting the law-jobs done. These entail focusing on 'mediation, organisation, policing, teaching, scholarship' (Llewellyn, 1941, p. 7). For him, the lawyer's cognition of social functioning imposes a different legal education, not obsessed only by rules and principles. Far from denigrating doctrinal analysis and jurisprudence, Llewellyn advocated the study of law as a 'behavioural science'. This move had far-reaching consequences for the association of law only with the state: 'to make behaviour in the legal aspects of life the subject-matter of a "science" is to overcome the obsession that *only the State* can have significance in this connection, and so to open up the closely comparable phenomena of primitive law in primitive society, and of sub-group "by-law" within our own society' (Llewellyn, 1941, p. 8). Overall, as William Twining (2012, p. 190) has noted, the focus on behaviour should not be read as an endorsement of behaviourism in psychology or functionalism in sociology. Rather, it should be understood as a plea for a more inclusive (and perhaps eclectic) juristic method open to empirical as well as anthropological research and, therefore, closer to socio-legal research than Romano's juristic approach.

Nonetheless, Llewellyn's approach to legal order maintains a special focus on its material dimension, both methodologically and substantially. The internal relation between formation of social groups and institutional ordering is always present in all his major works. Llewellyn's specific contribution to this issue for legal scholarship is not a version of legal realism but an anthropologically inclined approach to legal studies that may rightly be part of the canon of legal materiality studies.

3.2 Second Variation: Integrative Institutionalism

This second section will broach two main versions of legal institutionalism that have been put forward at around the same period by Rudolph Smend and Costantino Mortati. Given that the Weimar's experience and the Italian Fascist regime represent their context, they both share similar concerns about societal formation in conditions of friction between the multiplication of social forces and the rise of authoritarianism (see Wilkinson, 2021). They have both resorted to the same logic for facing this issue, that is, the logic of integration of social fragments or relations into the legal order. Furthermore, they have found in the process of *constitutionalisation* the best instrument for integration. In brief: this stream addressed the question of materiality with the ultimate aim of stabilising the social order in the absence of homogeneity and recognising that the best instrument for obtaining that homogeneity is integration into the legal order. While both authors acknowledge the challenge posed by pluralism, they face it by looking for mechanisms to contain pluralist fragmentation. In other words, integration is their answer to the proliferation of different autonomous and semi-autonomous social spheres whose pull has centrifugal effects on political and legal unity. The relevance of their work for determining the materiality of the legal order cannot be overestimated as their influence has extended beyond the academic sphere and has shaped powerful judicial functions in Germany and Italy, either directly through their thinking or because of the work of their students. However, the medium of integration imagined by these two thinkers is different and this leads to diverging understanding of the notion of materiality itself.

The first author whose work is paradigmatic for this version of legal institutionalism is Rudolph Smend. The gist of his contribution has to be seen in the idea that the legal order is an integration process that boosts or protects social homogeneity and crucially achieves it without resorting to the exercise of force. His main concern is to avoid a situation where a loss of organic links within society (owing to the rise of the multi-class state, that is, a social order inhabited by people with different class-backgrounds) has a destructive effect upon the unity of the state. This concern is based on *material grounds* because the loss of organic links produces distortive and unhealthy dynamics (of psychological and sociological nature) between the individual and the community. Reflecting on his own intellectual development, Smend would later remember that the originating factor of the integration theory was 'the sight of the political chaos of the sickly constitutional state of the 1920s, out of which emerged a desire to offer in contrast the original healthy sense of the constitution' (Korioth, 2000, p. 210). Only a dynamic conception of the legal order can ensure that this 'sickly constitutional state' will eventually recover. However, Smend gives a particular twist to that dynamic and grounds his analytical starting point in the psychological level of the individual conscience. The stability of the legal order depends largely on the psychological convictions of the individual in relation to the wider community.

All of this points to an expansive definition of the legal order as it has to account for the integrative process:

> The constitution is the legal order of the state, or more precisely, of the life through which the state has its reality 147 – namely, of its process of integration. The meaning of this process is the constantly renewed production of the totality of the life of the state, and the constitution provides the legal norms for various aspects of this process (Smend, 2000, p. 240).

Smend recognises that the legal order is based on norms, but it cannot be only that. It is also reality, a statement that implies that the legal order ought also to include the material life that is constantly reproduced and integrated in the constitutional order. In this sense, Smend is clear in stating that the 'constitution as integration' is a process and not a static thing: 'This doctrine is incompatible with each attempt at substantialising the constitution ... but it is also incompatible with the characterisation of the constitution as a static and immobile order' (Smend, 2000, p. 241). The reproduction of the state legal order is similar to a daily plebiscite, given that the state 'exists only because, and as long as, it integrates continuously, with and in individuals' (Smend, 2000, p. 218). Fundamentally, the aim of integration is to produce and then stabilise the political unity of the state. There is no other content or aim for integration. In other words, the process of integration is functional to the constant amalgamation of the social formation into an encompassing state legal order. This thought is coherent with Smend's idea that the state is an end in itself and neither has nor needs any external source of legitimacy. However, the state's legal order cannot be conceived in static terms because otherwise the order would collapse or disintegrate. In fact, against Kelsen (and other positivists), integration requires a constant dialectic between the individual and societal order, a dialectic that revolves around those aspects of life that have to be integrated. As Kelsen noted, however, Smend loosely and at times even formally defines life aspects, and this remains one of the weak spots of his theory (Kelsen, 1930, pp. 26–7). Their centrality is part and parcel of Smend's anti-formalist approach. In fact, integration does not take place in the formal constitution, but mostly (even though not exclusively!) at the level of the real or material legal order.

But what exactly is the content of the process of integration? Smend is definitely more interested in capturing the logic of the process rather than its content. In his main work, *Constitution and Constitutional Law*, published in 1928 (the same year of Schmitt's *Constitutional Theory*), Smend drew a distinction among three different types of integration: personal, functional, and substantive or material (*Sachliche*). *Personal* integration is not reducible to the ideology of 'leaderism' (*Führertums*), but it is related to the organisational aspect of the social order. Smend assumes that there is no social order without relations of command and obedience. The role of the leader or the chief is to perform a symbolic function, enabling individual recognition within the communal dynamic. Not every personality qualifies for the role, but Smend is not worried about technical capacities. What counts for him is the capacity of the leader to perform a unifying function. Moreover, personal integration operates at many levels, both macro and micro: it is realised not only by the supreme institutions of the state but by non-institutional exceptional personalities and the bureaucracy as well (judges included).

The second type of integration is *functional* because it is linked to forms and procedures that are supposed to mobilise the emotions of the subject. Functional integration takes place through two modalities: one is contractualist, and in European legal orders is equivalent to the procedures of parliamentary politics. This represents a channel of an integrative battle for whose occurrence only a general and rather unspecified set of values is required. On the contrary, the other modality of functional integration is linked to domination (*Herrschaft*), grounded either in irrational values that provide the legitimacy basis or in rational ones that are justified as administration (hence, they are based on a technical form of knowledge). Smend has a clear preference for the parliamentary modality because the modality of domination presupposes a background of stable common values. Domination cannot manage properly situations of deep social conflict and value pluralism. The parliamentary system has the advantage of being less demanding in terms of its preconditions, and it ensures the dynamism of the process of integration. According to Smend, it does not matter whether parliamentary politics produces good decisions: 'what matters is whether the parliamentary dialectic within the parliament and among the citizenry leads to group formation, association, creation of a specific common political attitude' (Smend, 2000, pp. 225–6). Personal and functional integration share one common trait: they are both formal and purposeless (that is, they do not pursue a concrete aim).

Material integration takes place around certain values that are necessary for consolidating personal and functional integration. While it would not be correct to rank these forms of integration, it is evident that the material one works as the glue by virtue of which the state legal order is held together. Part of the effectiveness of common values lies in their 'symbolic manifestation' (Landecker, 1950, p. 44). A key passage in Smend's masterpiece describes the vital role of the legal order for the development of the state. In fact, the state 'is not a real entity in itself, which is then used as a means to actualize external goals. Rather, it has actuality at all only to the extent [that] it is an actualization of meaning; it is identical with this actualization of meaning' (Smend, 2000, p. 229). The real constitution materialises the existence of the state and makes the latter solid and permanent. Yet, this does not mean that Smend dismisses the idea of state sovereignty. The state remains a superior legal order for two reasons: first, unlike other associations, its existence is not dependent upon external powers; second, it has the capacity to integrate itself 'merely by dint of an inherent logic of values into an integrating system gravitating toward itself' (Smend, 2000, p. 243).

From this standpoint, Smend's main work points to a couple of legal instruments as shaping vectors of the process of integration. Smend articulates a theory (1) of fundamental rights and (2) of their constitutional interpretation as essential tenets of the integrative function. Against legal positivists, which would make interpretation a textual or originalist question, Smend considers this a reductive approach which reduces constitutional rights to the simple principle of government by law. Rights should not be conceived in the negative sense, that is, as shields against the potential encroachment of the state upon one's individual freedom. Smend argued that rights are crucial because they represent vectors for the continual renewal of the state's will. Instead of being a limitation of power, they are foundational instruments of the state's power. However, their integrative function should not be confused with an inclusionary mechanism. Of course, in a sense, by integrating, fundamental rights can also include subjects into the political community. But integration is not universal and its symbolical and cultural dimensions are actually drawing boundaries around the community. For example, when describing the catalogue of fundamental rights contained in the second part of the Weimar constitution, Smend notes explicitly that their purpose is to enhance the *feeling* of German communal identity. Therefore, fundamental rights came to perform a double role in Smend's thinking. On the one hand, they would serve as a limiting device with exclusionary force. This would enhance the unity of the legal order. On the other hand, they would revive public life and resist the stagnation of collective convictions (Van der Walt, 2014, p. 266). Unlike the liberal separation between society and the state's legal order, the integration theory presents a holistic approach to the two terms (society and state) by explaining the quality of integration as a dynamic whole that constantly subsumes its individual parts in different spheres (cultural, legal, social). Fundamental rights are transformed into an active agent of homogeneity-building: they do not enable individual autonomy, but they encourage the syncretism of individual conscience and communal values. Their interpretation becomes the core practice of building up the materiality of the legal order. The dynamic behind the application and extension of fundamental rights is ultimately one of integration into the legal order.

Mortati's legal theory rests firmly within the tradition of legal institutionalism. His work – which spans from the 1930s to the 1970s – is heavily indebted to Romano's, from whom Mortati took the idea that the main unit of legal analysis is the legal order. More specifically, the insight that is borrowed from Romano is that the legal order is an institution, or set of institutions, understood as a constellation of organisations united by an objective, goal, or principle. Therefore, an institution is first of all an organised unity (with different degrees of cohesion) which contains essential normative elements. However, the aims or goals that animate the legal order should not be conceived in deontological terms: rather, they are teleological aspects of the legal order. As we shall see, these aims or goals organise the materiality of the legal order.

According to Mortati (1998), law can take up any content. The specificity of a legal norm (against social or moral ones) can be found not in its content but in its normativity, which is (as we shall see) closely associated with its enforceability. Under this aspect, Mortati's institutionalism is not categorically different from classic legal positivism. And as is the case for most versions of legal positivism, the normativity of legal norms is based on a specific function: consolidating or stabilising the social order by helping with the achievement of certain fundamental aims. What is distinctive about Mortati's legal theory is its insistence on the link between societal formation and legal ordering. Of course, it is possible to separate for analytical purposes societal formation and legal ordering, and even to treat them as distinct units, but the jurist ought always to bear in mind that this is an *internal relation*, that is, the legal order does not grow or emerge from outside of society. Rather, creation of the legal order is already embedded in societal formation and development, and vice versa.

It is better to clarify that Mortati's intention is not to extract a sociological approach to law out of legal institutionalism. And this is not because Mortati despises sociological approaches to law. It is possible to observe societal factors intertwined with the development of the legal order. However, this concerns only sociological knowledge and not, strictly speaking, juridical knowledge. If Mortati had stopped at this consideration, he would have adhered to the classic legal positivist distinction between sociology of law and legal philosophy. His project points to a different direction because the jurist ought to focus on the internal relation between social formation and the legal order as the proper juridical foundation:

> [t]he jurist does not do sociology, because she does not look out for the factors that determined the rise of forces and ideologies on which the state is based; nor does she express any opinion about them. By tracing the features that are necessary for conducts and social relations to acquire legal significance, she delineates the facts that emerge out of these very relations as they unfold within a given order. (Mortati, 2007, p. 128)

In brief: it is one thing to study the relation between society and the legal order from a sociological perspective with a view to becoming aware of the natural, material, and cultural factors that have brought together a social group and to assess the congruence between formal legal structures and social reality; it is quite another thing to look for those social elements that already contain seeds of legal normativity. The jurist's task is to penetrate social reality in order to find those internal elements that will integrate the formal legal order.

Organisation is the central motive of Mortati's legal institutionalism and the jurist has to focus on it in order to track the fundamental pillars of the legal system. Mortati insists in particular on two key tenets of his legal institutionalism: (1) institutions do precede, at least logically, the system of norms because (2) they intrinsically contain their own order organised around a telos or finality. Point (1) establishes that norms become legal precisely because they are embedded in an institution. Point (2) comes as consequence of (1): an institution is an already organised unity whose identity is given not by its ever-changing norms but by the aim or telos animating it. Norms can change, but the identity of the legal order remains the same. The requirement of an organised unity entails that roles and functions within that unity have been already distributed: this is the process of differentiation. Within a social group, differentiation requires ordering processes (that is, normative facts) and ordered structures (that is, constituted authorities). Hence, the constitutive elements of the legal order, that is, its organisational and normative building blocks, are: (a) the ensemble of the subjects linked by common interests that require co-operation for their realisation (in a nutshell: one or more social groups); (b) the presence of an authority that can objectify a legal will applicable to all the members of the group; (c) one aim or a system of fundamental aims; (d) a system of social relations juridically qualified; (e) an array of means (normative and not) through which legal certainty is established (mostly in virtue of enforcement). It is worth pausing and examining briefly these elements by bearing in mind that they all have to be present to form the legal order. The first one refers to the subjects whose interests and needs constitute the reason for the association in the first place; the second postulates that the group is internally structured and recognises some members as holding special positions; the third establishes the teleological nature of legal orders by assuming that each and every institution is created or brought about for an instrumental reason, that is, to realise certain goods or values; the fourth and the fifth elements, concerning, respectively, interaction among subjects and the means to govern it, require a system of legal norms. The latter point needs a supplement of explanation. Legal norms are distinguished from the other types of norms (norms of etiquette, moral norms, and social norms) because they are fundamentally imperative. According to Mortati, the imperative character of norms contains two aspects: first, positive law is in the end reducible to a command that influences human conduct and, second, this feature of law threatens a sanction or the loss of an advantage or privilege, in case of disobedience. The command is not autonomous and categorical (as it is in the Kantian moral law) but heteronomous and parasitical on the interests of the subjects to comply or not. This is where Mortati remains distant from the 'generative institutionalists': the imperative character of norms is part of the process of consolidating a certain level of social homogeneity so that law seems to be called to contain rather than facilitate social processes of law-making.

A further clarification on the nature of legal orders is necessary. Being built on institutions, Mortati's legal theory is in principle open to the recognition of the plurality of legal orders. As there are infinite interests (of the general, common, and individual kind) and needs, there must also be a multiplicity of possible legal associations. Yet, Mortati's real concern is not with the growth of this type of pluralism. Even relationships among institutions (and legal orders) can be organised, and often are, by differentiating among their functions and aims. Such differentiation also introduces a hierarchy that is part and parcel of a wider legal order. In fact, legal orders (and therefore institutions) can be of different kinds, of which Mortati sketches a tentative chart. A crucial distinction is between legal orders with a single and specific aim, and legal orders with general aims (which can still be divided into voluntary and involuntary orders). Orders with only one specific aim can be socially, culturally, or morally oriented (charities or sports associations, for example). Here, Mortati is not fully explicit, and it remains uncertain whether each and every order with only one finality can really qualify as juridical. Possibly the lack of clarity comes with his lack of interest in the issue. Nonetheless, Mortati is adamant when he addresses those legal orders with general fundamental aims, which are qualified as political orders. These are defined as political because general aims (for example, maintenance of peace among different social groups) can in principle address almost any interest or need as long as it is functional to the pursuit of the fundamental aim. In other words, the aim can be encompassing. These political legal orders can be original (*sui juris*) when they derive their nature internally or from a relation of dependence on another superior order (derivative orders such as, in the modern state, regions or provinces). The former are sovereign legal orders as well. Sovereignty means that the authority intrinsic to the legal order can found its origin in an internal principle of order that is not imposed from the external world. As a consequence, within its jurisdiction, this type of legal order remains hierarchically superior to the others. Central to this reconstruction is the ordering principle internal to each original legal order. Such a principle (or series of principles) necessarily operates under certain conditions, otherwise it would not perform its proper function: as already mentioned, it cannot be derived from the external world, but it has to be immanent to societal organisation; in the moment of forming the legal order, it bestows upon it some of its defining traits; the ordering principle operates also in the moment of integrating the system of norms, that is, when it becomes necessary to integrate new norms because of gaps or lacunae in the legal order; in other words, in the moment of guaranteeing legal certainty and legal stability, which is actually a self-limiting moment as the ordering principle limits itself according to the aims that the legal order is supposed to pursue.

Another basic aspect of Mortati's institutionalism has to be added at this point. According to him, a legal institutionalist approach paves the way for a *concrete* study of the legal order, that is, a study centred on its organisational aspect and the differences and articulations that pertain to it. It should be noted that Mortati found Romano's theory rather abstract and vague on this point. While Romano was clear on the priority of the organisation over the norm, he did underestimate the internal ordering properties of each organisation. Each institution, according to Romano, is moved by a vital principle, but, the objection goes, this principle 'c[ould]not perform its function . . . if it did not have the character of uniformity and constancy, that is, if it were not a norm; this norm would be without any doubt different ... from those disciplining directly behaviours, but still similar in its function' (Mortati, 1998, p. 46). In this passage, and in others, Mortati seems to hint at a type of reflexivity of the social order that anticipates the reflection of societal constitutionalism. The material dimension of the legal order can be put into proper shape only by applying a higher level of norms to the norms organising social differentiation.

Comparison with a scholar belonging to a different tradition of studies can be useful to appreciate the importance of secondary norms in Mortati's understanding of the materiality of the legal order. Confrontation with Kelsen's pure theory of law is essential to the formation of Mortati's thought. According to Mortati, Kelsen has put forward the wrong solutions, but he has asked some relevant questions. For Mortati, the biggest issue is Kelsen's methodology, especially because it limits the epistemic boundaries of legal knowledge. Mortati cannot accept the pureness of the pure theory. This is the case despite the fact that the pure theory presents precious insights. For example, the idea of the basic norm should not be discarded entirely. The problem, for Mortati, lies in the way the basic norm is conceived by Kelsen. While it is laudable to try to anchor the legal order to an objective point of reference, for Mortati it is not helpful to understand the basic norm in terms of an hypothesis. Conceived in this way, the basic norm cannot perform its epistemic role. This is because its epistemic value is limited to legislative production: in fact, a hypothetical basic norm cannot extend to the sphere of discretion or the sphere of interpretation because only those norms that descend logically from another norm belong to the legal system. Moreover, a basic norm that is conceived as hypothetical cannot contribute to identification of the main distinctive characters of the legal order. Therefore, even when there is a substantial change of the fundamental tenets of a legal order, the basic norm as hypothesis does not register it as relevant for legal knowledge. The mere command 'obey to the supreme organ' is too unspecified from an epistemic perspective because it is possible that the same organ would change dramatically without any legal registration of the change. Therefore, Mortati was firmly convinced that, to make sense of the basic norm, the legal theorist ought to begin by taking into account fundamental social relations (Mortati, 1998, p. 41). In this way, the basic norm operates not as a precondition of the conceivability of the legal order but as the validity-condition for it. Mortati believes that, to function as a condition of validity, the basic norm has to be effective as well. For this reason, when writing about constituent power, Mortati adopts the idea of *normative fact* to describe the organised social interactions that give rise to a new constitutional order (Mortati, 2020, p. 39): a normative fact contains its own law and the guarantees for its own persistence in time. Constituent power is not a force that is exercised socially for bringing the legal order into existence while remaining external to it. Accordingly, two precious lessons can be learnt from engagement with Kelsen: (1) observing fundamental relations cannot be deemed immaterial to the legal theorist; and (2) the existence of the legal order as 'it emerges from the observation of the facts is a necessary element for attaching the property of legality to the norms' (Mortati, 2007, p. 88), but it does not assume a distinctive value from that of validity and becomes relevant, so to say, only a posteriori. In the end, Mortati believes that Kelsen's thesis ought to be turned upside down. The normative order has to be deemed to be valid if it is efficacious as well. It follows that the root of the normative system should be looked for in social reality. More specifically, undergirding a normative order one always finds a social relation that operates as a source of juridification. But if the social relations bearing the normative order are structured and already contain normative elements, why should they be left outside the realm of legal knowledge? Such a move allows Mortati to put at the centre of his legal theory the relationship between the constitution of society (the real constitution) and the legal constitution (the juridical one), by reframing the way social facts and norms interact and become productive. It should be added that the two notions do not belong to different spheres of reality.

Normative facts are not self-standing norms, but in Mortati's view they need a bearer. The coupling between the societal dimension of organisation and the formation of the legal order that is achieved by normative facts is obtained by virtue of the mediation of the political system, or at least of a set of political subjects that support it. As Mortati, like Smend, operates under the assumption, at least, that general legal orders are possible only in the presence of political unity, it becomes essential to explain how unity is achieved and maintained. This becomes even more urgent when differentiation produces proliferation of social groups. Political unity is what allows preservation of the materiality of legal orders. Without it, there would be only unmanageable conflict. Only political parties are capable of providing a *trait d'union* between societal organisation and the unity of the state legal order. This is because they maintain a relation but at the same time preserve the distance between the social and the state. They are also capable of organising their activities according to general aims or goals that, by definition, cut across all different spheres of society. Political parties are organisations with ordering principles whose force is exercised internally (through organisation of the party) and externally (through society and the state). In brief, political parties, like Machiavelli's new prince, ensure that their political aims radiate in the direction both of social organisation and of consolidation of state unity (cf. Rubinelli, 2019). The political party is an institution of synthesis because it constructs political unity out of the differentiation of society. Therefore, it is also the main engine of integration:

> It [the party] is here understood in a more specific conception as that association – endowed with a general view encompassing the life of the State in all its aspects . . . Political parties are pushed to shape into an organisation that, despite the personal autonomy of their chiefs, put as the predominant element a general political idea . . . capable not only to hold together the group that assumes it, but also to represent a centre of attraction for new adherents and the conquest of State power. (Mortati, 1998, p. 71)

Such a conception of the role of the party is not exclusive to an authoritarian society. Mortati applies it to a multi-party system as well. What is central in his conception is the idea that the process of integration happens via one specific medium: organised politics. This is the case because, otherwise, the process of social differentiation, left to itself, would not generate a stable legal order. Nonetheless, the role of the law remains central. In fact, the general aims that political parties pursue and inscribe in the legal order enjoy legal relevance from the very beginning. So, while the engine of integration is political, its form remains fundamentally legal.

There is coherence in Mortati's method because the centrality of organised political parties is just a reflection of the idea that the materiality of the legal order is ultimately a matter of organisation. Like other legal institutionalists, Mortati embraces organisation as the key formative process of the legal order. However, he gives to politics a prominent role as the organisational system *par excellence*. While this might have been an accurate description of certain forms of constitutional orders post-World War II, where political parties effectively played a decisive function (at least in some countries), it is doubtful that it can account for the growth and complexity of social organisation in contemporary times. Mortati's option might still be supported as a normative option (i.e., only a political process can obtain a fair organisation of society), but descriptively it does miss important aspects of social development and fragmentation. This is possibly the weakest aspect of his thinking as it seems to exaggerate the capacity of political will to shape society, with the risk of falling back into political theology. The problem with this understanding is that it reduces societal formation to an act of political will and obscures the energies and the conflict that permeate fundamental social relations.

4 The New Materialism

The institutionalist stream reviewed in the previous section did not produce an evident and self-proclaimed heir. It is not the task of this Element to spot the reasons for such a fragmented legacy, however. Candidates are multiple. A plausible reading of systems theory and societal constitutionalism (cf. Blokker and Thornhill, 2017) interprets these as heirs of legal institutionalism (Golia and Teubner, 2021). According to this interpretation, the relationship between the legal system and other social systems has been thought of in more functionalist terms because it has been conceived as a structural coupling among different social subsystems in order to stabilise each of them. A certain degree of continuity between legal institutionalism and systems theory can indeed be imagined. In both approaches, organisation is a central phenomenon and institutions articulate the relations between societal formation and legal ordering. But societal constitutionalism does not thematise the materiality relation. The closest the systems-theory approach comes to addressing the question is in terms of an external reference to the environment. For this reason, despite its rich and enlightening take on the formation of modern societies, the systems-theory approach is not directly relevant for this Element.

　　In the contemporary debate, the most straightforward attempt at addressing the materiality relation in legal orders can be found in Actor-Network Theory (from here on, ANT; see McGee, 2019). The status of materiality is at the centre of ANT's research agenda; for this reason, ANT is often included in a wider constellation of 'new materialisms' together with object-oriented ontology. The new materialisms put the object at the core of their analysis of ontological knowledge and agency (Harman, 2018). While in many modern attempts at tracking societal formation, representation and construction of the social order were deemed its constituent parts, the new materialisms put matter itself as an active part of social (and non-social) relations. Objects can be apprehended without mediation, and they also enjoy forms of agency that feed back on the observer. This is the case because there is no ontological gap between things and their representation (Meillassoux, 2009). Hence, new materialisms support a form of flat ontology, where there are connections and interactions among objects, but not hierarchies and dualisms. By developing an inclusive materialism, that is, a materialism that includes everything, ANT rejects the old materialism of the Marxist type. There is no privileged or foundational form of agency and no permanent structure of society. Moreover, by focussing on appearances, ANT denies the existence of levels of reality. From this perspective, the materialist distinction between material reality and ideology is unacceptable. More generally, ANT rejects the notion that there is a substance that persists below appearances and that guarantees the identity of objects. Objects' identities are determined by relations, not substances. Under this aspect, ANT bears unintentional similarities with the generative strand of legal institutionalism, but it provides a more sceptical and provocative view of the concept of social order. As its name eloquently evokes, ANT is not focussed on systems and environments, and, as we shall see, it denies that the idea of the 'social' can be reduced to a totality or an aggregation of individuals (Latour, 2006, pp. 153–4), but it does include an original conception of materiality that diverges dramatically from previous streams. The starting point of ANT is a denial that there is something like a social order. Bruno Latour notoriously said that 'there is no whole or parts' (Latour, 1984, p. 183). Rather, there are material processes of patterning that follow a logic of punctualisation (Law, 1992). This logic drives associations among objects. There is no intrinsic identity behind their composition. Their materiality is based on contingency and their formation lasts until they can no longer resist the forces of attraction of other associations.

Unlike that of legal institutionalism, ANT's epistemology does not accept any form of reductionism concerning social knowledge: the distinction between subject and object, the priority of the whole over its parts, the recognition of different levels of reality (micro, meso, and macro), the ontological difference between the individual and the institution. The reality of the world (it is difficult to refer to social reality given Latour's suspicion about it) is conceived by Latour as a set of relations among singular events. The basic unit of reality is indeed the *relation*; units are woven together as a web of intricate relations among nodes (Croce, 2020, p. 18). It is fundamental to note that there is no categorical difference between 'nature' or 'environment' and the social, so that ANT's understanding of reality cuts across the spectrum of traditional disciplines. Even though reality appears as the interaction between individuals or substances that bear a certain level of permanence, ANT maintains that this view hides the relational nature of every actor-network:

> All phenomena are the effect or the product of heterogeneous networks. But in practice we do not cope with endless network ramification. Indeed, much

of the time we are not even in a position to detect network complexities. So what is happening? The answer is that if a network acts as a single block, then it disappears, to be replaced by the action itself and the seemingly simple author of that action. (Law, 1992, p. 385)

The capacity of networks to act together does not entail a different social ontology: a network should still be observed as a concretion of a set of relations among nodes. As a consequence, the social ontology expounded by ANT is also alternative to many conceptions of the social order. In this sense, ANT's materialism is alternative to the previous two streams examined in this Element. While for the Marxist tradition the material aspect of the social and legal order is intrinsic to the relation between human labour and nature, and for legal institutionalism it is an essential feature of the organisation of society, ANT's flat ontology propounds an expansive and inclusive conception of materiality. ANT's materialism does not know of social systems or basic hidden structures: reality is flat because there is no preordained order but, rather, a process where an unforeseeable number of actants[10] converge or associate and produce a series of effects. Agency happens not in hierarchical structures but in the articulation of forces that associate and disassociate. The dynamics of association do not fall prey to naïve realism or naïve idealism; they revolve around a point that becomes organised into a functional unity. The logic behind such unity is conceived in topological terms: it is the most densely connected element in the network and it comes to serve as an 'obligatory passage point' (Callon, 1986, p. 205).

In Latour's (2006) account, materiality is at the forefront of the observer's concerns and knowledge. It is an essential relation for grasping how nodes (and, among them, institutions) are formed. Indeed, the formation of the 'social' is a question of network ordering. It should be highlighted that network ordering is always a relational activity and cannot be compared to a static achievement. Networks are made not only of humans but of a myriad other objects. Social relations and institutions are clusters of this mediated interaction. In brief, societal networks cannot be reduced to interactions between humans and, at a more complex level, institutions. A whole series of non-human materials is involved in the composition of each artefact (see the brilliant example of the door handle in Latour, 1992, pp. 225–7). This, then, is the crucial analytical move made by ANT theorists: the suggestion that the social is nothing other than patterned networks of heterogeneous materials. In other words, an organisation (or a concretion of an actor-network) would not be possible were it not for a process of interaction among a multiplicity of material elements. Hence,

---

[10] This is a technical term in Latour's philosophy, inspired by Greimas' linguistics: an actant is anything (animate or inanimate) that contributes to agency by acting or being acted upon.

the idea that ANT proposes a 'new materialism' that is not limited to relations among humans but includes other materialities as well.

But ANT does not stop there: it pushes the idea further by bringing into the picture the so-called hybrid actant, which is the product of an interaction between an animate object and an inanimate one. More specifically, Latour is interested in the material agency of these hybrids as agency is not intrinsically human but, rather, a composition of different materialities. There are no social objects, only hybrids in Latour's ontology. Agency is given not by the social context (which for Latour remains too vague to be an object of scientific knowledge) but by a set of elements that stretches out into the network of materials that surrounds each hybrid. Therefore, contrary to system theory's position, agency cannot be limited to social systems (see Teubner, 2006, p. 505). Also, hybrid actants do not need to be capable of communication and reflexivity; however, they still need to possess a capacity of association. Things are not intrinsically agents; rather, they point to relations and processes of composition because they are the objects that make those processes visible and traceable. Their materiality is constituted not just by the matter of the objects but, rather, by 'the kind of agency that is afforded by, elicited from, or ascribed to them' (Pottage, 2012, p. 168); it is the outcome of the composition of human and non-human elements. Composition is the key concept here: a politics of composition is what Latour suggests as the main approach for understanding what we have defined as societal formation. Its materiality is therefore not static but a constant composition and re-composition of networks and networks of networks. This compositionist approach does not reduce aggregates to their components, but, at the same time, it does not deny that each actor is a network made of other networks. In all of this, a great merit of ANT is to avoid the causal explanation of how networks come to be formed. It is the case neither that the human aspect shapes and organises networks (for example, through labour) nor that it is objects (machines, texts, institutions, etc.) that determine the shape of the network through technological determinism. Both views treat the human and non-human dimensions of the social order as two separate heaps. What determines what, however, is at best an empirical question for ANT, and it is a question that cannot be solved a priori, but only by observation. In brief, this approach casts a granular (or molecular) view on the emergence of social formation and, accordingly, of legal institutions.

Given these premises, one can see that legal institutions and persons are not the outcome of a centralised process of social organisation but are always already imbricated in networks and act as mediators of other processes of assemblage or disaggregation. In this scheme, an actor is what it is on the basis of the force of the relations that link it to other actors. It is then possible to translate the activity of ordering into one of assembling actor-networks. More accurately, ordering is an activity that requires the translation of heterogenous materialities. And the materiality of the order is the materiality of an assemblage of networks. Equally importantly, it is also the materiality of the legal conductors (classically, but not exclusively, for law it is the case of documents such as statutes, decrees, and judicial decisions). The focus of the observer has to be on the process or the effects of network organisation (and not on what is assumed to be an accomplishment) because social ordering is not an achievement but a site of struggle among many actor-networks. Hence, 'the bits and pieces assembled into an order are constantly liable to break down, or make off on their own' (Law, 1992, p. 387).

What is the specific role of law in the operations of assemblage of the social? In a nutshell, law is a way of assembling the social through legal materials. When it comes to law's function, Latour (2002, p. 283) becomes even more explicit: 'Law is autonomous in relation to social because it is a means of producing the social, of articulating and contextualising it, but it has no specific domain or territory'. But, in fact, Latour (2005, pp. 34–5) is less interested in differentiation than in composition: with a plastic metaphor, Latour mentions that institutions such as religion, science, and law are mingled indistinctly like 'the veined marble panels of the Basilica di San Marco in Venice, in which no figure is clearly recognizable' (Latour, 2005, p. 34). Each of these institutions has its own modality of existence and, according to the observer, can become dominant in any given configuration. In this respect, the social dimension of the actor-network is given by the peculiar point of observation of one of these institutions. Law is a particular way of assembling the social because it is less 'technical' than the others as it is a *mode of enunciation*; second, law is self-descriptive, that is, the identification of certain enunciations as legal is achieved by reference to a criterion that is posited by those enunciations themselves. Accordingly, it is not a subject that enunciates the law but a heterogenous assemblage of actors, both material and semiotic (McGee, 2015, p. 35). The materiality of the social order can be found abundantly in law as there is 'more "society" in law than there is in the society that is supposed to explain the making and operation of law' (Latour, 2002, p. 278, quoting the French Roman law historian Yan Thomas). Hence, we are advised that 'law juridifies all of society, which it apprehends as a totality in its own particular way' (Latour, 2002, p. 281).

The difference with legal institutionalism here becomes palpable: according to Latour, a legal institution is not the mediation among different spheres of the social order, precisely because their mode of existence is not one of a sphere, domain, or region, but that of a network. To study a legal institution entails carving out from the networks that compose it the vectors that preserve its existence. Indeed, networks depend on a multiplicity of materials for their solidity and durability, such as, for example, morality, politics, technology, economy, but, at the same time, modes of transmission of actual law (Latour, 2005, p. 37). Institutions are effects of processes of translation of heterogenous materials into patterning and social orchestration. Any institutional formation entails overcoming a set of resistances and for this reason it is possible to strategise about translation of materials as part of an assembling process.

To determine the materiality of the legal order, it is essential to understand how an enunciation can be recognised as legal and not political, economic, or religious. Latour's view of law as a regime of enunciation is captured with great efficacy by a lively description contained in his seminal study of the French Conseil D'Etat:

> Imagine a game of Lego in which the traditional attachment by means of four studs is replaced by attachments of many different kinds. Imagine then that each of these attachments makes further attachments either easier or more difficult. Now assume that in this somewhat peculiar game of LEGO some blocks are connected by means of a LAW connector and others by means of a POL connector ... Give the game to some kids to play with. They will produce forms – institutions – which will have longer or shorter segments which we can call LAW because they are connected by means of a LAW attachment, even though a given block might also, in another segment, be joined by means of a POL attachment. Of the multi-coloured assemblage that is produced, one might say, depending on the intensity of the connections, "that, more or less, is law" and "that, more or less, is politics". (Latour, 2005, p. 40)

The legal order does not have a 'specific domain or territory' and it is imbricated in a set of networks whose internal links are made possible by connectors of different nature. Therefore, legal institutions are 'more or less' law, although they also contain political and economic connectors. At this point, it is quite instructive to compare ANT with a systems-based approach, bearing in mind that Latour openly rejects the autonomy of law as a legal system. According to ANT theorists, there is no strict separation between actor and environment. But, as a second important difference, precisely because it is not possible to separate system and environment in coded terms, Latour already takes for granted the law as a mode of enunciation and reconstructs it not according to a binary code, as in systems theory, but in terms of gradients or processes (Pottage, 2012, p. 177). Thus, ANT does not thematise the fact that the legal relevance of any event is always at stake and does not present itself as self-evident. This is rather problematic as law does not come in ready-made blocks of legality that can work as connectors among events (legal or not); ANT presents the law as a univocal marker and legal institutions are a set of networks whose organisation is formed by overcoming a series of resistances generated by heterogenous materials that do not lend themselves easily to being assembled. Hence, institutions are the association of materialities within which law plays a predominant connecting function. In a nutshell, one could say that ANT gives an account of the materiality of legal institutions in associative terms (through a set of strategies of translation for overcoming resistance). But, despite its centrality, the logic of association remains under-theorised. Emphasis on the non-representational character of associations does little to account for the patterns of clustering they exhibit. Thinking of associations in topological terms (by stressing the presence of nodes or points) does not do much to explain the force at work that marshals the other elements in the network around it. The risk of this way of describing the work of associating as formative of materiality is that it begs the question of what stuff are the connections that form an association made. Furthermore, the flat ontology of ANT does not have much to say about what propels the patterning of certain connections rather than others (Tellmann et al., 2012, p. 212). Without theorising the orientation that pervades the logistics of associations and connections, it is difficult to understand the ability of a network to achieve functional coherence (Appadurai, 2011, p. 536). Yet, it is clear that certain patterns tend to be formed more frequently and more automatically than others.

5 The Study of the Materiality Relation

The previous sections have offered an overview of certain approaches to legal philosophy that have tried to bring the materiality question to the forefront of the analysis. An essential aspect common to most of those reflections is the idea of looking at the engines of societal formation and verifying how the legal order is implicated not as an external force but as embedded into social relations. Revealingly, each of the three main streams that have been identified corresponds to periods of change in the social-economic structure of the Western world: the rise of industrial capitalism (materialism); corporatism and the New Deal (legal institutionalism); the interweaving of industrial production with financial capital (new materialism). Each of these turns has also identified a peculiar technique of organisation: division of labour among classes; social integration through legal and constitutional means; assemblage or association of networks.

A central thesis running as a thread through the sections of this Element is that social organisation and, more specifically, the organisation of relations of production and reproduction are (also) juristic activities: they are intrinsically interwoven with the form and content of the legal order. A legal philosophy that wants to address the materiality question cannot avoid taking up analysis of the legal order's political economy. The streams of legal philosophy broached in the previous sections can still provide important entry points into the question of the organisation of the political economy, but it will be necessary to take into account their limits. In the current academic context, there are signs of a new attention to the relation between law and the political economy. This is partially owing to the limits of the dominant Law & Economics paradigm, which cannot provide a material methodology because (1) it is based on methodological individualism and (2) it has investigated, mostly, how law could be used to enhance the economy. In a nutshell, Law & Economics was not designed to be sensitive to the materiality of the legal order.

Against this background, other works have emerged in the last decade, especially in the USA (coming not only from legal philosophers but from commercial and public lawyers as well), which point to a different method-ology, that is, towards a retrieval of the political economy of the legal order as the field where materiality is formed and shaped, that is, where materiality can be retrieved by legal knowledge.[11] This is part of a wide umbrella that goes under the name of Law & Political Economy (LPE), but it should be added that it does not signal a return to standard materialism. Really, LPE's main worry is the dangers caused by the blind spot of modern legal theory, represented by lack of consciousness of the organisation of the political economy. In this preoccu-pation, it is possible to hear an echo of Polanyi's concern for the disembedding of the political economy from society and its impact for the stability of demo-cratic legal orders.

Although LPE is intellectually still a movement in its early stage, a version of it with some level of theoretical systematicity has been offered in the last decade by a group of authors (Deakin et al., 2017; Pistor, 2019) directly inspired by the first wave of institutionalist economists of the likes of Thomas Veblen and John Commons. This type of institutionalism should not be confused with the legal institutionalism presented in Section 3; rather, this 'new legal institutionalism' is more indebted to the first version of economic institutionalism and, more specifically, to the recognition of the constitutive relevance of legal instruments for setting up capitalist relations. John Commons (1995, pp. 12–46), for example, famously analysed how the jurisprudence of the US Supreme Court at the end of the nineteenth century forged a conception of private property that became essential for the development of US capitalism.

---

[11] Poul Kjaer (2020, p. 11) notes that central to the law of the political economy is how to look at society: whether through the lenses of holism or differentiation.

Like economic institutionalists, the new legal institutionalists do not present themselves as proponents of a general theory of law; rather, they aim at explaining how modern societies (i.e., mature capitalist societies) are constitutively organised by and through legal institutions. Explanations of the relation between law and the capitalist organisation of economic activities are at times depicted as the outcome of evolutionary achievements by spontaneous forms of regulation or customs. This resonates with a conventionalist account of the development of social and legal orders. Yet, according to new legal institutionalism, this is deemed to be an unsustainable view of the role of law in complex modern societies: 'In legal institutionalism, then, law is treated as more than custom: it is primarily constituted by the state' (Deakin et al., 2017, p. 190). One could add: law does not evolve conventionally, but primarily out of authoritative decisions. This new legal institutionalism denounces both the reductionism of the materialist explanation of capitalist societies and that of neoclassical economics with its view of the legal order as a necessary transaction cost. Understanding the materiality of the legal order entails, for new legal institutionalism, the recognition of two ontological claims: first, and beyond controversy, the law of a capitalist political economy is always a mix of private and public legal instruments. Within this horizon, the element of coercion granted specifically by state law is still extremely important in shaping economic and social relations. Second, law is not only an expression of power but a *constitutive* aspect of power (Deakin et al., 2017, pp. 188–9). The framing capacity of law makes it power-generative: law, according to the new institutionalists, by framing social relations decides also on the distribution of power across them. The end result of this approach is to turn the relation between societal formation and legal ordering upside down. It is legal ordering that allows for the constitution of capital as a social relation. Social rules are recognised as important ordering factors, but the key difference is made by state positive law. Ultimately, the law sets the conditions of existence for fundamental relations of the political economy. In contemporary times, this is achieved by the dual component of the law involved in constituting social relations. While state-based law grounds the formation of social relations, the code used to shape the latter is based in private law and in forms of spontaneous ordering. For this reason, institutionalists speak of legal 'hybridity' (Pistor, 2013, pp. 322–3), which is internal to the legal code itself (public/private).

The constitutive thesis advocated by the new legal institutionalism entails that social reality is created by law not just as a self-description of itself but as the constitution of social reality, at least in its economic dimension. There seems to be no social remainder beyond the legal description. In this way, materiality ultimately disappears as the law and its coercive powers are placed in a self-referential position without any link with other social factors. This position implies a certain degree of malleability of legal norms as well. Their assemblage and re-combination are feasible because they are just forms, relatively unconstrained by the social context. Hence, formal legal norms ought to be the main object of study and, also, of policy reforms. From this perspective, legal knowledge is not particularly problematic. Lawyers and officials can participate in the construction of the social reality of economic interaction by interpreting or, as increasingly happens, by creating law (for example, through the drafting of contracts by transnational law firms: Pistor, 2019, ch. 1).

The problem affecting this version of LPE is that the notion of a constitutive relation is under-theorised and, in the end, assumed rather than explained. The notion of the constitution of the political economy by law fails to account for the fact that what new legal institutionalists understand as legal institutions (contract, property, trust, money, and the state itself) are not just legal notions. Property and contract, for example, are not created by law out of the blue, and they maintain an element of materiality by being embedded in certain social practices among which economic practices are perhaps the most important. In other words, the normativity of property and contract is not exclusively legal but economic as well. This consideration can be extended to many other legal institutions. Nonetheless, there is an important intuition behind the LPE's project which should not be sidelined too quickly. The study of a legal order's political economy can be instrumental to the tracking of its materiality because it covers fundamental and general (meaning: spanning across a vast spectrum of) activities for the formation and maintenance of the social order. It is the task of the lawyer to observe the legal elements or traces contained in those organisational processes. The study of the materiality relation should focus on these concrete processes of productive organisation to look for the traces of the legal order that they contain in themselves.

Although the study of societal organisation of production is central to understanding the materiality of the legal order, there is preliminary theoretical work that still needs to be done. It is indeed difficult to take up the latter task if the notion of a materiality relation has not been clarified. A clear concept of relation and of its role in social organisation is necessary as a first step in understanding the specificity and the nature of the materiality relation. Hence, besides the study of the legal order's political economy, attention in the study of materiality should also be paid to the concept of relation. Here, the study of materiality ought to investigate the contemporary debate in metaphysics. More specifically, the study of materiality should be aware of two debates concerning, respectively, the nature of relations and the notion of the legal relation. There is much to learn from these two debates with a view to clarifying the status of the materiality relation.

The starting point is the recognition that the study of the materiality relation is, first of all, a metaphysical question. The way the enquiry is framed is of extreme relevance for the study of materiality. Whether the relation between social facts and the legal order is described as a gap or not has obvious epistemic consequences for the study of materiality. If there were a gap, the study would have to find a bridging mechanism that would allow the observer to understand the relation between the two relata.[12] But, perhaps even more importantly, a crucial question is to establish whether, in the materiality relation, the relata have more, less, or the same weight as the relation itself (see, for an introduction to the debate, MacBride, 2020). Another connected and relevant question is whether the relation, as it is stated forcefully by Ontic Structural Realism (Ladyman and Ross, 2007),[13] is ontologically more fundamental than the relata themselves, and whether the metaphysical notion of fundamentality (on the question of the fundamental level, see, for an introduction, Schaffer, 2003) can help in gaining some traction in the understanding of the materiality relation. Finally, one of the crucial tasks of the study of materiality is to determine whether the relation of materiality is one of causation, supervenience, or grounding (see, for an overview of metaphysical relations, Rea, 1996; Marmodoro and Yates, 2016).

The study of the materiality relation will also have to thematise its legal status. For this reason, it is opportune to extend the enquiry to the notion of the legal relation. The contemporary debate on the legal relation gravitates around the discussion on metaphysical relations, but it cannot be fully absorbed into it. Its focus is on the conditions that define social interaction as legal. Broadly speaking, there are two alternative versions of the legal relation. One identifies seeds of legality in social interaction without requiring the presence of legal institutions (Schumann, 2008; Pavlakos, 2020; Somek, 2020). Legal relations obtain with enabling moral facts against non-relevant coercion and the enabled grounding fact of interaction of agents. Legal obligations, under this view, arise out of the combination of legal relation and the formation of legal institutions. The alternative version understands the legal relation as the relation that holds between agents by virtue of the conditions set by positive law plus the facts of

---

[12] Most likely, this would mean recognising the materiality relation as an external relation: see Armstrong, 1997, pp. 87–9.

[13] This view is usually adopted with the purpose of avoiding the problems affecting the substance-based metaphysics of individuals. But it does not deal with another possible metaphysical monist position, which does not give a prominent role to relations: for this last view, see, for example, Schaffer, 2010.

interaction involving physical and mental facts. According to this interpretation, legal relations are legal obligations. Institutionalisation becomes a condition for enabling the formation of legal relations. Far from being exclusive to one stream of legal thought (see, for example, Finnis, 2011, p. 204), this latter view is certainly compatible with the position expressed by the new institutionalists.

In light of the previous remarks, we can conclude that the agenda for the study of materiality is twofold. On one hand, it is necessary to zoom in on the details of the fundamental relations that make up legal orders under the conditions of the contemporary political economy. On the other hand, a clear understanding of the metaphysical nature of those relations is a theoretical precondition for an accurate study of materiality. Only the parallel pursuing of these two lines of analysis can capture the material dimension of the legal order.

References

Agamben, Giorgio (1998). *Homo Sacer: Sovereign Power and Bare Life.* Stanford, CA: Stanford University Press.

Appadurai, Arjun (2011). 'The Ghost in the Financial Machine'. 23 *Public Culture* 517–39.

Armstrong, David (1997). *A World of States of Affairs.* Cambridge: Cambridge University Press.

Blokker, Paul, and Chris Thornhill (eds.) (2017). *Sociological Constitutionalism.* Cambridge: Cambridge University Press.

Bogdanov, Alexander (2022). *Tektology: Universal Organizational Science.* Amsterdam: Brill.

Brown, Wendy (2015). *Undoing the Demos.* New York: Zero Books.

Callon, Michael (1986). 'Elements of a Sociology of Translation: Domestication of the Scallops and the Fishermen of St. Brieuc Bay', in John Law (ed.), *Power, Action, and Belief: A New Sociology of Knowledge?.* London: Routledge, pp. 196–233.

Christodoulidis, Emilios (2021). *The Redress of Law.* Cambridge: Cambridge University Press.

Christodoulidis, Emilios (2022). *Functional Differentiation.* Cambridge: Cambridge University Press.

Commons, John (1995). *Legal Foundations of Capitalism.* London: Routledge.

Croce, Mariano (2018). 'Whither the State? On Santi Romano's *The Legal Order*'. 11 *Ethics and Global Politics* 1–11.

Croce, Mariano (2020). *Bruno Latour.* Rome: Derive Approdi.

Croce, Mariano, and Andrea Salvatore (2013). *The Legal Theory of Carl Schmitt.* Abingdon, UK: Routledge.

Croce, Mariano, and Andrea Salvatore (2022). *Carl Schmitt's Institutional Theory.* Cambridge: Cambridge University Press.

Deakin, Simon, David Gindis, Geoffrey M. Hodgson, Kainan Huang, and Katharina Pistor (2017). 'Legal Institutionalism: Capitalism and the Constitutive Role of the Law'. 45 *Journal of Comparative Economics* 188–200.

Epstein, Brian (2015). *The Ant Trap.* Oxford: Oxford University Press.

Finnis, John (2011). *Natural Law and Natural Rights.* Oxford: Oxford University Press.

Girard, René (1972). *Violence and the Sacred.* Baltimore, MD: Johns Hopkins University Press.

Girard, René (1986). *The Scapegoat*. Baltimore, MD: Johns Hopkins University Press.

Golia, Angelo, and Gunther Teubner (2021). 'Societal Constitutionalism: Background, Theories, Debates'. 15 *Vienna Journal of International Constitutional Law* 357–412.

Halbertal, Moshe (2011). *On Sacrifice*. Princeton, NJ: Princeton University Press.

Hardin, Russell (1999). *Liberalism, Constitutionalism, and Democracy*. Oxford: Oxford University Press.

Hardin, Russell (2013). 'Why a Constitution?', in David Law and Mila Versteeg (eds.), *Social and Political Foundations of Constitutions*. Cambridge: Cambridge University Press, pp. 51–72.

Harman, Graham (2018). *Object-Oriented Ontology*. London: Pelican.

Hart, H. L. A. (1994). *The Concept of Law*. Oxford: Clarendon Press.

Hauriou, Maurice (1970). 'The Theory of the Institution and the Foundation', in Albert Broderick (ed.), *The French Institutionalists*. Cambridge: Cambridge University Press, pp. 93–124.

Hunter, Rob (2021). 'Constitutional Law and the Capitalist State', in Paul O'Connell and Umut Özsu (eds.), *Research Handbook on Law and Marxism*. Cheltenham, UK: Edward Elgar, pp. 190–208.

Itzcovich, Giulio (2020). 'Something More Lively and Animated Than Law'. 33 *Ratio Juris* 241–57.

Jessop, Bob (2015). *The State*. London: Polity Press.

Kahn, Paul (2004). *Putting Liberalism in Its Place*. Princeton, NJ: Princeton University Press.

Kelsen, Hans (1930). *Der Staat als Integration: Eine prinzipielle Auseinandersetzung*. Dordrecht: Springer.

Kjaer, Poul F. (2020). 'The Law of Political Economy: An Introduction', in Poul F. Kjaer (ed.), *The Law of Political Economy: Transformation in the Function of Law*. Cambridge: Cambridge University Press, pp. 1–30.

Korioth, Stefan (2000). 'Introduction', in Arthur Jacobson and Berhnard Schlink (eds.), *Weimar: A Jurisprudence of Crisis*. Los Angeles: University of California Press, pp. 207–12.

Ladyman, James, and Don Ross (2007). *Every Thing Must Go*. Oxford: Oxford University Press.

Landecker, Werner S. (1950). 'Smend's Theory of Integration'. 29 *Social Forces* 39–48.

Lassalle, Ferdinand (1942). 'On the Essence of Constitutions', in *Marxist Archive*, www.marxists.org/history/etol/newspape/fi/vol03/no01/lassalle.htm.

La Torre, Massimo (2010). *Law as Institution*. Dordrecht: Springer.

Latour, Bruno (1984). *Les Microbes*. Paris: La Découverte.

Latour, Bruno (1992). 'Where Are the Missing Masses? The Sociology of a Few Mundane Artifacts', in Wiebe Bijker and John Law (eds.), *Shaping Technology/Building Society*. Boston, MA: MIT Press, pp. 225–58.

Latour, Bruno (2002). *La fabrique du droit*. Paris: Éditions la Décourverte.

Latour, Bruno (2005). 'Note brève sur l'écologie du droit saisie comme énonciation'. 8 *Pratiques cosmopolitiques du droit* 34–40.

Latour, Bruno (2006). *Reassembling the Social*. Oxford: Oxford University Press.

Law, John (1992). 'Notes on the Theory of Actor-Network'. 5 *Systems Practice* 379–92.

Lenin, Vladimir (2002). *Materialism and Empiriocriticism*. Forest Grove, OR: Pacific University Press.

Lewis, David (1969). *Convention*. Oxford: Blackwell.

Lindahl, Hans (2019). *Authority and the Globalisation of Inclusion and Exclusion*. Cambridge: Cambridge University Press.

Llewellyn, Karl (1934). 'The Constitution as an Institution'. 34 *Columbia Law Review* 1–40.

Llewellyn, Karl (1940). 'The Normative, the Legal, and the Law-Jobs'. 49 *Yale Law Journal* 1355–1400.

Llewellyn, Karl (1941). *My Philosophy of Law*. New York: Julius Rosenthal Foundation.

Llewellyn, Karl (2008). *The Bramble Bush*. Oxford: Oxford University Press.

Loughlin, Martin (2003). *The Idea of Public Law*. Oxford: Oxford University Press.

Loughlin, Martin (2017). *Political Jurisprudence*. Oxford: Oxford University Press.

MacBride, Fraser (2020). 'Relations', in Stanford *Encyclopedia of Philosophy*, https://plato.stanford.edu/entries/relations/.

Marmodoro, Anna and David Yates (eds.) (2016). *The Metaphysics of Relations*. Oxford: Oxford University Press.

Marmor, Andrei (2001). *Positive Law and Objectivity*. Oxford: Oxford University Press.

Marmor, Andrei (2008). *Social Conventions*. Princeton, NJ: Princeton University Press.

Marmor, Andrei (2011). *Philosophy of Law*. Princeton, NJ: Princeton University Press.

Marx, Karl (1976). *The German Ideology*. New York: Progress Publishers.

Marx, Karl (1980). *Grundrisse: Selected and Edited by David McLellan.* London: Palgrave.

Marx, Karl (1991a). *Capital.* Vol. 1. London: Penguin.

Marx, Karl (1991b). *Capital.* Vol. 2. London: Penguin.

Marx, Karl (1996). *Early Writings.* London: Penguin.

McGee, Kyle (2015). *Bruno Latour.* Abingdon: Routledge.

McGee, Kyle (2019). 'Law in the Mirror of Critique', in Emilios Christodoulidis, Ruth Dukes, and Marco Goldoni (eds.), *Research Handbook on Critical Legal Theory.* Cheltenham, UK: Edward Elgar, pp. 238–58.

Meillassoux, Quentin (2009). *After Finitude.* London: Bloomsbury.

Mortati, Costantino (1998). *La costituzione in senso materiale.* Milan: Giuffré.

Mortati, Costantino (2007). *Una e indivisibile.* Milan: Giuffré.

Mortati, Costantino (2020). *La teoria del potere costituente.* Rome: Quodlibet.

Negri, Antonio (1984). *Marx Beyond Marx.* South Heatley, MA: Bergin and Garvey.

Pavlakos, George (2020). 'Redrawing the Legal Relation', in Jorge-Luis Fabre Zamora (ed.), *Jurisprudence in a Globalized World.* Cheltenham, UK: Edward Elgar, pp. 174–94.

Pistor, Katharina (2013). 'A Legal Theory of Finance'. 41 *Journal of Comparative Economics* 315–30.

Pistor, Katharina (2019). *The Code of Capital.* Princeton, NJ: Princeton University Press.

Polanyi, Karl (2001). *The Great Transformation.* Boston, MA: Beacon Press.

Postema, Gerald (1982). 'Coordination and Convention at the Foundation of Law'. 11 *Journal of Legal Studies* 165–203.

Pottage, Alain (2012). 'The Materiality of What?'. 39 *Journal of Law and Society* 167–83.

Rawls, John (1971). *A Theory of Justice.* Boston, MA: Belknapp Press.

Raz, Joseph (1990). *Practical Reason and Norms.* Oxford: Oxford University Press.

Rea, Michael (1996). *Material Constitution: A Reader.* Lanham, MD: Rowman & Littlefield.

Romano, Santi (2017). *The Legal Order.* Abingdon, UK: Routledge.

Romano, Santi (2019). *Frammenti di un dizionario giuridico.* Rome: Quodlibet.

Roughan, Nicole (2019). 'The Official Point of View and the Official Claim to Authority'. 38 *Oxford Journal of Legal Studies* 191–216.

Rousseau, Jean-Jacques (1994). *The Social Contract.* Oxford: Oxford University Press.

Rubinelli, Lucia (2019). 'Mortati and the Material Constitution'. XL *History of Political Thought* 515–47.

Schaffer, Jonathan (2003). 'Is There a Fundamental Level?' 37 *Noûs* 498–517.

Schaffer, Jonathan (2010). 'Monism: The Priority of the Whole'. 119 *Philosophical Review* 31–76.

Schmitt, Carl (2006). *The Nomos of the Earth*. New York: Telos Press.

Schumann, Fredrick (2008). 'The Appearance of Justice: Public Justification in the Legal Relation'. 66 *University of Toronto Law Journal* 189–223.

Shapiro, Scott (2011). *Legality*. Boston, MA: Harvard University Press.

Smend, Rudolph (2000). 'Constitution and Constitutional Law', in Arthur Jacobson and Berhnard Schlink (eds.), *Weimar: A Jurisprudence of Crisis*. Los Angeles: University of California Press, pp. 213–47.

Somek, Alexander (2020). 'Legality and the Legal Relation'. 33 *Ratio Juris* 307–16.

Spaak, Torben (2018). 'Legal Positivism, Conventionalism, and the Normativity of Law'. 9 *Jurisprudence* 319–44.

Spinoza, Benedict (2000). *Ethics*. Oxford: Oxford University Press.

Tellmann, Ute, Sven Optiz, and Urs Staeheli (2012). 'Operations of the Global: Explorations of Connectivity'. 13 *Distinktion: Scandinavian Journal of Social Theory* 209–14.

Teubner, Gunther (2006). 'Rights of Non-humans? Animals and Electronic Agents as New Actors in Politics and Law'. 33 *Journal of Law and Society* 497–521.

Teubner, Gunther (2012). *Constitutional Fragments*. Oxford: Oxford University Press.

Thornhill, Chris (2011). *A Sociology of Constitutions*. Cambridge: Cambridge University Press.

Trivisonno, Alexander Gomes (2021). 'On the Continuity of the Doctrine of the Basic Norm in Kelsen's Pure Theory'. 12 *Jurisprudence* 321–46.

Tronti, Mario (2019). *Workers and Capital*. London: Verso.

Twining, William (2009). *General Jurisprudence: Understanding Law*. Cambridge: Cambridge University Press.

Twining, William (2012). *Karl Llewellyn and the Realist Movement*. Cambridge: Cambridge University Press.

Van der Walt, Johan (2014). *The Horizontal Effect Revolution and the Question of Sovereignty*. Berlin: De Gruyter.

Vinx, Lars (2021). 'Kelsen and the Material Constitution of Democracy'. 12(4) *Jurisprudence* 466–90. DOI: 10.1080/20403313.2021.1921493.

Wilkinson, Michael (2021). *Authoritarian Liberalism and the Transformation of Modern Europe*. Oxford: Oxford University Press.

Wydra, Harald (2015). *Politics and the Sacred*. Cambridge: Cambridge University Press.

Cambridge Elements ☰

Philosophy of Law

Series Editors

George Pavlakos
University of Glasgow

George Pavlakos is Professor of Law and Philosophy at the School of Law, University of Glasgow. He has held visiting posts at the universities of Kiel and Luzern, the European University Institute, the UCLA Law School, the Cornell Law School and the Beihang Law School in Beijing. He is the author of *Our Knowledge of the Law* (2007) and more recently has co-edited *Agency, Negligence and Responsibility* (2021) and *Reasons and Intentions in Law and Practical Agency* (2015).

Gerald J. Postema
University of North Carolina at Chapel Hill

Gerald J. Postema is Professor Emeritus of Philosophy at the University of North Carolina at Chapel Hill. Among his publications count *Utility, Publicity, and Law: Bentham's Moral and Legal Philosophy* (2019); *On the Law of Nature, Reason, and the Common Law: Selected Jurisprudential Writings of Sir Matthew Hale* (2017); *Legal Philosophy in the Twentieth Century: The Common Law World (2011)*, *Bentham and the Common Law Tradition*, 2nd edition (2019).

Kenneth M. Ehrenberg
University of Surrey

Kenneth M. Ehrenberg is Reader in Public Law and Legal Theory at the University of Surrey School of Law and Co-Director of the Surrey Centre for Law and Philosophy. He is the author of *The Functions of Law* (2016) and numerous articles on the nature of law, jurisprudential methodology, the relation of law to morality, practical authority, and the epistemology of evidence law.

Associate Editor

Sally Zhu
University of Sheffield

Sally Zhu is a Lecturer in Property Law at University of Sheffield. Her research is on property and private law aspects of platform and digital economies.

About the Series

This series provides an accessible overview of the philosophy of law, drawing on its varied intellectual traditions in order to showcase the interdisciplinary dimensions of jurisprudential enquiry, review the state of the art in the field, and suggest fresh research agendas for the future. Focussing on issues rather than traditions or authors, each contribution seeks to deepen our understanding of the foundations of the law, ultimately with a view to offering practical insights into some of the major challenges of our age.

Cambridge Elements ≡

Philosophy of Law

Elements in the Series

Printed in the United States
by Baker & Taylor Publisher Services